The Confessions of a Capitalist

Ernest Benn

THE BOUVERIE LIBRARY

The Confessions of a Capitalist

by

ERNEST BENN

"... Those effects of an economic cause which are not easily traced are frequently more important than, and in the opposite direction to, those which lie on the surface and attract the eye of the casual observer.

"This is one of those fundamental difficulties which have underlain and troubled the economic analysis of past times; its full significance is perhaps not yet generally recognised, and *much more work may need to be done* before it is fully mastered."

—MARSHALL.

ERNEST BENN LIMITED
LONDON

Large Print Edition published 2014 by Skyler J. Collins.
Visit: www.skylerjcollins.com

Originally published in 1925.

ISBN-13: 978-1495944826
ISBN-10: 1495944824

Foreword

WHEN these *Confessions* first appeared in 1925, the capitalist system was being subjected to ever-increasing criticism and calumny. It has taken three periods of Socialist government to stem the tide, and to cause many people to examine afresh the principles on which our former prosperity was based. The rate of government expenditure and some other figures mentioned in this book have increased enormously since it was written, and the case for private enterprise has, I believe, been strengthened by nearly everything that has happened in the past twenty years.

To bring this edition within the compass of the Bouverie Library, a series initiated by my eldest son, I have agreed to omit a chapter on America which appeared in earlier issues. Nothing has altered my impression that capitalism has attained its highest level in that enlightened country, and indeed my conclusion in 1925 has a new significance in relation to the circumstances of 1948. " The world," I then wrote, " has nothing to fear from American leadership. This challenge to mankind is a very different thing from that which came from Napoleon or from the Kaiser. America . . . will lead in service, in example of a higher standard, in the making of ever-increasing wealth. That is the class of leadership, which, provided others follow or better still, share in it, can bring nothing but good to the human race."

Yet no outside aid can replace the self-help which alone can save our country, and it is my earnest hope that, in helping to explain the workings of private enterprise to a new generation, this book may encourage that spirit of personal risk and endeavour which never fails to show itself among Englishmen in a time of adversity.

Oxted, March, 1948.   E. B.

Preface to the First Edition

THREE things may be said about this book upon which there must, I think, be general agreement, and I mention them to save my critics trouble.

The first is that the book is in bad taste, dealing as it does with matters which, by common consent, are not usually written or talked about. Secondly, the book aspires to no literary merit. The matter of it has been dictated in the manner of commercial correspondence and no attempt has been made to shield bald fact behind art or style. And thirdly, the book and the arguments it contains are decidedly materialistic. That is not because I am unconscious of the ethical side of all these problems, but because I am concerned for the moment with the more practical aspect of affairs.

I have endeavoured to put a point of view which is all too little considered in modern discussions, and without which, so it seems to me, all discussions of the common wealth must be futile and dangerous.

As will be obvious from the length and complications of the story, my obligations to others are too heavy and numerous to mention in detail. But the book could not have been written without the accomplished help of my secretary, Florence Robinson, or of G. L. Jarratt and B. H. Tripp. Nor would it have seen the light but for the kindly encouragement of my old friend, Sir Arthur Spurgeon, who was good enough to spare time to read the manuscript.

Oxted, September, 1925.   E. B.

Contents

I

INTRODUCTORY APOLOGY

I AM a business man, making and enjoying a very substantial income. I own two motor-cars. I live amidst surroundings that to many people would seem luxurious. I control a fair-sized business, and, directly and indirectly, I suppose I am responsible for the activities of about 2,000 " wage slaves." I am, in fact, the sort of person against whom the whole of the Socialist propaganda seems to be launched and, when I listen to current political discussion, I find myself regarded not only as a superfluity but as a bar to progress, as one of the causes of poverty, want, and distress.

My bookshelves are crammed with volumes explaining what an evil creature I am. I possess numbers of books telling me how beautiful the world would be if only I and my class could be eradicated. The literary case against me is indeed overwhelming. Ruskin says:

... But the greater part of such gain is unjust; ... Sin sticks so fast between the joinings of the stones of buying and selling, that " to trade " in things ... has warped itself, by the instinct of nations, into their worst word for fraud; ... and " trader," " traditor," and " traitor " are but the same word. ... While I have traced the finer and higher laws of this matter for those whom they concern, I have also to note the material law—vulgarly expressed in the proverb, " Honesty is the best policy." That proverb is indeed wholly inapplicable to matters of private interest. It is not true that honesty, as far as material gain is concerned, profits individuals. A clever and cruel knave will in a mixed society always be richer than an honest person can be. (*Commerce:* Munera Pulveris.)

Karl Marx sums me up in the following way:

The money-owner strides in front as capitalist; the possessor of labour power follows as his labourer. The one with an air of importance, smirking, intent on business; the other, timid and holding back, like one who is bringing his own hide to market and has nothing to expect but—a hiding. (*Capital*: Vol. I, Capitalistic Production.)

Modern writers are no less definite in their views about me.

" The capitalistic system . . . " says Mr. Philip Snowden, " has waged war and sacrificed unnumbered lives for commercial gain " (*Labour and the New World*), and further makes reference to " The competitive struggle in which the fittest to survive are those endowed with cunning, greed, and audacity."

Mr. Sidney Webb is even more direct:

" The process of distribution," he says, " developed by the profiteering system might more fitly be described as an elaborate system of interception and blackmail." " The Labour and Socialist movement of the world is essentially a revolt against the capitalist system of society." " The primary purpose of the Socialist is to focus attention on the peculiar kind of tyranny now exercised . . . by a relatively small class of rich men over a mass of poor men." " It is unnecessary to dwell in greater detail upon the poverty of the poor as the most obvious evil result of the ' free enterprise ' of the profit-making capitalist." (*The Decay of Capitalist Civilisation*.) " But the central wrong of the capitalist system is neither the poverty of the poor nor the riches of the rich; it is the power which the mere ownership of the instruments of production gives to a relatively small section of the community over the actions of their fellow-citizens and over the mental and physical environment of successive generations." (*A Constitution for the Socialist Commonwealth of Great Britain*.)

All this is boiled down at the street corner to straightforward robbery, and every night at a thousand meetings the argument is reduced to terms of the vernacular. But the political agitation against my class is not to me so serious as the greater mass of middle-class opinion which, partly from a sympathy with the sentimental side of Socialism and partly from a species of snobbery, adopts with unanimity an attitude of mind definitely unsympathetic to commerce. Even many of those who are prepared to accept the idea that buying and selling is a proper occupation are not able to go to the length of believing that great wealth acquired in this way is a creditable achievement. The man with a big income is definitely at a discount. The public does not quite believe that he is altogether honest, and even his friends will entertain the suspicion that there is a " wangle " somewhere. There seems, in fact, to be little doubt in the mind of anybody that the accumulation of big fortunes in individual hands is bad for society. Public opinion has accepted almost without question the fallacious theory that riches are made at the expense of others. It is not necessary in England to declare oneself a Socialist to adopt the view that there is something wrong with the system, for Socialist agitators and Christian preachers vie with one another in denunciation of the existing scheme of things. Socialism has grafted itself on to our public opinion so completely that even at a Tory meeting it is possible to raise a laugh at the expense of the man like myself with £10,000 a year. The clergy not infrequently look upon his charity as conscience money, and the working classes regard him as their oppressor.

In case it may be thought that I am unduly sensitive, or am exaggerating in this matter of public opinion and wealth, I quote an answer which was given in the House of Commons as recently as February, 1924, by the then Lord Privy Seal, Mr. J. R. Clynes:

" I should have thought," said Mr. Clynes, " it was the aim of all political parties to effect by means of social legislation a more equitable distribution of wealth."

That reply was given by the then Leader of the House with the object of placating his hearers and demonstrating the sweet reasonableness of the Labour

Government and its sympathy with the parties to which it was opposed. That reply was received by the House with general agreement, and shows how completely we have accepted the notion that it is the duty of our legislators to effect this " more equitable distribution of wealth." It throws an interesting sidelight on the state of the public mind. I venture the opinion that there were not more than a score of persons present in the House of Commons (and I do not forget the whole of the Conservative Party) who felt that this statement of Mr. Clynes was a tragedy instead of a pious expression of the opinion of all parties. To me the attempt to redistribute wealth by legislation is a farce and a sham, for while it appears on the surface of things to be effective, it does not in reality have any such result.

It is easy to destroy wealth by legislation, and the human race is poorer, and human needs are still unsatisfied largely by reason of the great quantities of wealth that have been eliminated in this way. But to make wealth, or to redistribute wealth, by any process but the action of the individual is, so it seems to me, both ineffective and uneconomic. Thus, when I hear of political parties agreeing that they will build houses for the working class, I only see the supply of houses becoming ever shorter and shorter. When I read of the politicians settling the unemployment problem, I only think of the large numbers who will be thrown out of work by any such plans. I know what the politicians have done in other matters, such as the Irish question, and I am not anxious to see houses, employment, and other such vital things made the sport of political discussion for generation after generation, eventually to go the way of all political questions. I indulge in this little outburst against the politicians in order to bring out as clearly as possible the position in which I stand, and to throw into relief the great difference between my point of view and that of so many of my fellow-citizens.

Unlike the ordinary anti-Socialist agitator, I blame quite definitely the business community for the state of mind into which the public has been allowed to drift. Business men have clung to the old tradition that politics and business are things apart, and have allowed political forces to work in almost complete ignorance of the facts concerning the very matters with which they have been dealing. That was all very well so long as politics were concerned with the Franchise, Education, Home Rule, or the Disestablishment of the Church. To-day, however, when politics are almost entirely concerned with business matters, that attitude must be abandoned.

Everybody is now talking business, except the business man. The politicians, the doctrinaires, the parsons, the long-haired youths and short-haired maidens from the Universities, all have fixed views on industrial and commercial questions. Most of them are prepared to explain at a moment's notice how any piece of business should be conducted. From the smaller details right up to the higher organisation of industry there is nothing upon which they are not ready to express an opinion, the view expressed being, generally speaking, the more definite and exact in inverse ratio to the experience of its author. In all this dicussion the business man is silent.

I seldom talk about my business outside business circles. Indeed, in conformity with English social ideas, I am expected to forget it when I move in society. My neighbours know very little about it, and I know next to nothing about their business affairs. If I want to join a club, I strive to find some other qualification for membership than that of being a business man. When my children are entered for school their father is described as a " gentleman," or a " director of companies," or a " landowner," or anything but what he really is, because the best class of school does not like to think that it has any direct connection with trade. My business, like my underclothes, is a thing which, for some extraordinary reason, is barred from polite and interesting conversation. The urgent necessity, as it seems to me, for public enlightenment on matters of business has led me to put down on paper what I can remember of my business experiences and thus give, if possible, something in the nature of a substratum of fact to help future discussion. The task is not an easy one for many reasons. I am often impressed, when I listen to discussions on industrial affairs, to find how wide of the mark is most of the material that is contributed to them. Even in responsible quarters I find distorted ideas and much fundamental error, which cannot be explained but by an absence of such information as can be given only by the business classes—information which has hitherto been for the most part withheld. As a good example of thorough-going error, Ruskin's discourse on co-operation may be cited. Early in this he tells us:

> On the other hand, by the exact sum which is divided among them (*i.e.* the employees) more than their present wages, the fortune of the man who, under the present system, takes all the profits of the business, will be diminished." (*Time and Tide*, Letter i.)

Starting on that basis, Ruskin builds up the case for his particular form of co-operation and draws the reader on to the contemplation of a world of wealth and goodwill as from the summit of a high mountain. Had Ruskin had the advantage of a couple of years in a position of business responsibility, he would not have allowed himself to make a statement so completely false, much less have built up a case upon it.

In the fifty years of economic experience which we have enjoyed since Ruskin wrote, there is surely no one left who would be so innocent as to suggest that high wages necessarily reduce the profits of the employer. All the evidence points the other way.

Any exposition of sound economics labours under the disadvantage that it has nothing to offer—no prize to the poor, no comfort to the inefficient; a fact which probably explains the scarcity of sound economic literature. The Socialist writer, like the late Lord Northcliffe, has long ago discovered the wisdom of offering to the people what they think they want. Sound economic literature makes, therefore, no appeal to the passions or desires of the people as a whole. The poor do not read it, and the rich, as a class, make no effort to understand it. Thus it comes about that there are a hundred volumes on the theories of Socialism to every one on the theories of a sound society. It seems to me just possible—and this has weighed very heavily with me in the writing of this book—that the unattractive character of sound economic theories may find some compensating balance in the personal interest (if there is any) of such autobiographical details as I may be able to introduce. In this way we may succeed in getting a mixture with a flavour that will find acceptance with a public more numerous than those who are willing to read the orthodox economic treatise.

Science depends on fact as well as theory. The science of medicine would be a poor thing if it relied solely upon the theoretical. But the science of economics has been left almost entirely to the theorists. Except for Ricardo, I do not recall a single case of a man with much experience in the payment of wages who has ventured to write upon the theory of wages. I do not

B

know of any other case where a man who has made a large profit has contributed to discussions upon the theory of profit. I propose, therefore, to offer myself as a sacrifice, as it were, upon the altar of economic truth, to take my doings and examine them in the light of theory—a process which, it is my hope, may be found to be useful in these days when the economic structure of society should be the concern and study of all.

I am further encouraged to embark upon this self-imposed task by the folly of many of the efforts that are made to defeat Socialism. Socialism will not be killed by the exploitation of the " Red Bogey," by the appeal to the selfish instincts of those who happen to possess a little more than the average of this world's goods. That would seem to be obvious, if only for the reason that these persons are in such an insignificant minority. The discussion must be lifted above personal consideration. It does not matter a row of pins to society, considered as a whole, whether I retain my income or not; whether, as an individual, I continue to occupy my present position of responsibility. The only thing that matters is the well-being of the whole, the good of the greatest number. The only question for debate is whether others are damaged or benefited by my operations and the size of my emoluments. If it can be shown that my income could be taken from me and handed over to the unemployed, and that I could still live, and that the unemployed could live better by some process which had that effect, then the great majority of wealthy men would, I feel convinced, wave the Red Flag as vigorously and as enthusiastically as the most earnest Bolshevik. If, on the other hand, it is a fact, as I believe it to be, that my income is merely the index of the much bigger income enjoyed by a very large number of my fellow-men who, all of them, would lose such amenities as they now possess if my income were to go, then I have a case which must surely be examined, understood, and, if proved, accepted.

I am an unrepentant believer in private enterprise. I have failed to discover, in a long and diligent search, any material benefit which has ever reached mankind except through the agency of individual enterprise. I therefore regard the whole movement for creating wealth by political agencies as a snare and a delusion. For these reasons I see no essential difference between the Bolshevik of Russia and the numerous types of moderate Socialist. Both are committed to the abolition of private enterprise, and both are therefore destroyers of human comfort. The frantic efforts of the Socialist to exclude the Communist from the councils of the Labour Party are, to me, illogical and futile. I am reminded of two murderers who filled a good many newspaper columns a year or so ago. Their names were, I think, Bywaters and Thompson. Both directed their attentions to the same victim. The method of the one was to administer small doses of ground glass. The other adopted the more straight-forward and direct method of the dagger. The moderate Socialist is the ground-glass practitioner; the Communist uses the dagger. But, in so far as they are both bent upon the abolition of private enterprise, they are both murdering the chances of the human race to reach a higher standard of material comfort.

Nor are the difficulties of one who would defend the retention of wealth in individual hands made easier by the habit and customs of many wealth-owners. If my case rested upon what happens when a certain type of man secures £10,000 a year, what he does with it, how he lives, his home, his family, his personal surroundings, then I should throw in my brief at once. I would agree with the wildest revolutionary that the annihilation of a certain class of money-owner would remove an eyesore and a blemish from the social structure, provided such an operation could be performed without damage to the whole community.

For in pleading the case for individual wealth I have to grant the damaging fact that when wealth does get into individual hands it is often abused. There are persons of my own class who are much more responsible than Karl Marx for the spread of revolutionary ideas. I recently spent a week-end at a fashionable hotel at a health resort, and, if my three days' experience in those surroundings were all the information I had upon which to build a theory of social economy, I should find myself sympathetically examining Communism. The lounge of the establishment in question at tea-time on Sunday presented a picture of misapplied and wasted wealth impossible to justify or explain: women over- or under-dressed, oozing money, and giving from their conversation no trace of education or of finer feeling, and men whose main idea in life, judged again by what they said, seems to be how they can manage to get rid of the next five-pound note on some new form of excitement.

Do the " better class," using the term in its real sense, appreciate the fact that there are thousands of moneyed people spending wealth to no purpose, and giving generally an impression of the uses of wealth which is utterly false and extremely dangerous? These " wrong people " are at the back of half the discontent of which we hear so much. They live in public because no decent private society will have them. They are driven to the gold paint and crimson cushions of gaudy hotels because the more refined drawing-rooms of the educated are barred to them, and their every action is open to the inspection of the numerous

menials whose living they provide. Such persons form
for the agitator the typical " lady " and " gentleman."
The theories of taxation as expounded by the Socialist
are founded upon the idea that all wealth is spent in
this way, and when the worker hears of an income of
£10,000 a year he pictures to himself champagne, jazz-
bands, and motors with the appropriate uniformed
flunkey to assist in the enjoyment of each dissipation.
Yet, were it possible to examine the records of these
people, there is no question that in most cases their
wealth would be found to be derived from useful
industrial or commercial pursuits. Many of them are
the middle-class employers, who have succeeded in
organising industry and are keeping things going for
the benefit of us all. They take out of the common
stock no more than others are willing to pay for the
services which they render. Notwithstanding all their
waste and all the criticism which can be levelled against
them, they still represent the most economic method
yet discovered of carrying on the business of production and distribution. The charge which they make
upon industry, or the share of the product which they
take for themselves, is infinitely less than the charges
which would be involved in the establishment of any
other known organisation capable of taking their place.
The real remedy is by means of example and education
to lead them into better ways.

Notwithstanding, therefore, the difficulty of the task,
there are very urgent reasons why serious business men
should endeavour to set down their day-by-day experiences and the facts connected with their work for the
benefit of their fellows. One of these reasons was
brought very vividly to my mind recently in conversation with a well-known member of the first Socialist
Government, an earnest, honest seeker after good and
truth, as are most of these people. He mentioned to

me with unfeigned delight that the latest Treasury statistics disclosed the fact that there were now only 27,000 people left in the country with incomes of over £5,000 a year. I was told this with the same intonation as would be employed in discussing the number of bigamists or burglars or undesirable aliens. My friend was really convinced that the social millennium was all the nearer because of the diminishing number of persons with incomes of a respectable size. To him the cutting away of big incomes was helping to solve the troubles of the poor. To me this simple little fact was quite sufficient to explain the whole of the unemployment problem.

In venturing to discuss my private affairs as I do in the following pages, I am fully conscious of the grave risk that I run of failing to explain myself properly and of being misunderstood.

A difficulty of the kind that I have in mind was illustrated when discussing with a party of railway workers the cost of living index figures as a basis for wage settlements. I found it impossible to remove from the minds of my audience the suspicion that I was interested as a well-to-do person in keeping down their wages, and I failed, in a single evening's discussion, even to begin the winning of their confidence in my honesty. I am, further, running the risk that whatever I say will be controverted and disputed, not only by those who are anxious in the interest of knowledge and science to discover truth, but by those who have no other interests in life than the victory, or defeat, of some political party or faction.

As to that, I confess myself to be, with Professor J. R. Seeley, " One of those simpletons who believe that, alike in politics and religion, there are truths outside the region of party debate, and that these truths are more important than the contending parties will

easily be induced to believe. In both departments . . .
I watch with a kind of despair the infatuation of party
spirit gradually surrendering the whole area to dispute
and denial and despising as insipid whatever is not
controversial, until perhaps, at last . . . the brawl sub-
sides from mere exhaustion . . . suffering veritably
the catastrophe of Poland, which found such a fatal
enjoyment in quarrelling, and quarrelled so long, that
a day came at last when there was no Poland any more,
and then quarrelling ceased."

II

CHOOSING A CAREER

THE biggest problem that any family has to face is that of placing a young man in surroundings which will enable him to develop along his own lines and succeed in his own particular calling. This in most cases, although nine out of ten do not know it, is the rendering of satisfaction in some form or other to their fellow-creatures, or, in other words, finding self-expression through service.

I certainly began in a blind alley, with no definite duties except to do what I was told, with no training, and with few prospects except such as I could find for myself.

There is a deal of nonsense talked about " blind-alley occupations," and a quantity of money wasted in training-schemes which are inspired by this supposed evil.

To me, indeed, it is pathetic to see the money and effort that are spent upon training young people for work which, on arriving at years of discretion, they more often than not decline to do. This mistake is part and parcel of the fundamental error of the times in looking at work the wrong way round. In regarding the occupation as an end in itself, and considering only the convenience and the wishes of the worker, we to-day forget the very purposes of work. The consumer hardly exists in our minds. We have bandied and misused the word " service " until we have forgotten its meaning. I am inclined to think that in the early 'nineties we were a little nearer reality, and that the boys of that time did realise, though perhaps unconsciously, that they could never hope to make a success of life if they could not find some way of serving their fellows, and that their success would be great, or small, in proportion to the satisfaction that they would be able to give to others.

I am strengthened in these very unorthodox views by the fact that to-day I am supported by quite a number of colleagues of whom exactly the same may be said. A valued member of my Board of Directors responded to a notice that I put into our office window in 1897 announcing the fact that a boy was wanted. He was working the copy-press in a solicitor's office for a few shillings a week and did not find the satisfaction which his mind and soul were seeking in that process. It seemed to him that a boy's work in a publishing office might afford more scope, and his idea has proved right. A second colleague, who now occupies a very important position in the advertising world, was trained for the motor business, and a third was earning a poor living as an artist in decorated leather when he was attracted by the opportunities that publishing seemed to offer.

Definite training in some subjects is, of course, essential to the man who would follow one of the recognised professions. I am talking only of the preparation for what is to me the most delightful and most important of all the professions—the preparation for a business career.

My views are expressed by Mr. Selfridge in his book, *The Romance of Commerce*, when he says:

People must be governed, and there must be those who govern. Laws must be made, and there must be those who study, and those who execute these laws. People must be taught, and there must be teachers. All these, and the Church, the newspaper, the theatre, the fine arts,[1] are essential to the completeness of the State, to the happiness and safety of its people; but Commerce is the main stem, or trunk, where they are all branches, supplied with the sap of its far-reaching wealth. It is as necessary to the existence of any nation as blood to the physical man. That country in which trade flourishes is accounted happy, while that in which Commerce droops provokes shaking of heads and prophecies of downfall.

It would be absurd to pretend that, at the age of sixteen when I entered business, I was conscious of the many ramifications of the problem of choosing a career, but there is much satisfaction at the age of fifty in feeling that I did the right thing, and a complete absence of any regret at the decision which I then made. Mr. A. G. Gardiner, in the delightful book which he has written on the life of my father,[2] has told of the position of my family in the early 'nineties, and disclosed quite enough to show the need which existed for one of us to devote himself to business pursuits and to concentrate his attention on making money. I was, I think, as fully conscious of this need as a young boy could be, and it was that which weighed with me in pressing to be allowed to leave school and get to work.

I had up to that time been receiving an education which in these days would be regarded as altogether inadequate for any career. I was a pupil at the City Central Foundation Schools in Cowper Street, City Road, in the days before education had been so thoroughly nationalised, and when that fine institution with its 1,500 boys was still a semi-private, semi-charitable trust. My father being a ratepayer in the parish of St. Luke's, I was entitled to half fees, and the total cost of my education was covered by the sum of £5 a year. I did not do well at school. In all my years there I secured only one prize—a copy of *King*

---

[1] I should be inclined to put the fine arts on the border line of Commerce, and to regard the newspaper and theatre as Commerce pure and simple.

[2] *John Benn and the Progressive Movement.*

Solomon's Mines, awarded to me for " diligence." My father had given a free sketching entertainment to a literary society of which my form master was the honorary secretary. That set up an obligation which had to be balanced somehow and, there being no possibility of recognising my ability in any subject, " diligence " was made the excuse for including me in the prize list.

My career at Cowper Street was interrupted in the spring of 1889, just before I was fourteen years old, by eighteen months in France. The family income was not substantial enough to allow a normal period of education in a foreign country, but my father rightly held that a stay abroad was a thing to be desired, and, when the opportunity occurred to exchange my brother and me for two French girls without financial obligation on either side, he very wisely took advantage of it. My brother and I, he being twelve and I nearly fourteen, therefore found ourselves members of a bourgeois Parisian family named Bodson, who kept a small commercial hotel in the rue Caumartin, close to the Madeleine.

My father, whose fortunes were founded upon his pencil, was determined that we should both have a grounding in artistic matters, and particularly that we should become acquainted with the various styles in architecture and furniture. To this end we were enrolled at the art school of the VIIIme Arrondissement of Paris. We attended this school every evening, and there I really did win a prize which I valued. It not only seemed to point to some promise of ability in draughtsmanship in myself, but it also impressed me as a remarkable example of liberality in educational ideas on the part of the Parisian rate-payer, who was willing not only to provide a member of the French Academy to instruct an alien visitor, but even to award him prizes. After my stay in Paris I returned to Cowper Street and made an attempt to pass the London Matriculation, but without success. I failed in three out of the necessary five subjects. Judged, therefore, by any accepted standard in educational matters, I was a complete failure, and at Christmas, 1891, when I was sixteen and a half, I entered my father's office. I started to work as the junior office boy and served for a year under the senior office boy.

I was then put into the studio as a learner, my father still entertaining the idea with which he sent me abroad and hoping that I might develop into a draughtsman and designer. But a couple of years of pushing the pencil was enough for me. I don't think I succeeded very well, although my superiors were encouraging. My salary was 5s. a week, of which I saved 2s. 6d., living at home, within walking distance of my work. My total expenses were five dinners each week, which I took at the " Apple Tree " vegetarian restaurant in London Wall, where it was then possible to enjoy three courses for 6d.

I mention this saving of half my income because, as I shall explain at length in a later chapter, that is a fundamental part of my scheme of things. Ever since those 5s. days I have seldom permitted myself to spend more than half my earnings.

In those early days I used to think that I was worked fairly hard. At all events, hours were long. My father had then become Parliamentary candidate for St. George's-in-the-East, and I undertook the double duty of office work and assistant private secretary in political and public matters. Spending my days in Finsbury Square, I devoted my evenings to St. George's, returning regularly to our flat in Victoria Street by the 11.35 p.m. train from Shadwell to Westminster. That was the steady practice from 1892 to 1895. It will, therefore, be seen that every hour of the day was devoted to work, an arrangement which would be regarded, in the light of modern thought, as unhealthy and oppressive. But although the hours were long, we had not in those far-off times acquired the sense of speed and efficiency which is characteristic of the shorter hours of to-day. Office routine, for example, included a regular game of chess over the morning coffee.

After three years as office boy and assistant political agent, at the age of nineteen I was allowed to go off on the road as a traveller, selling advertisement space in my father's newspaper, *The Cabinet Maker*. In that capacity I worked hard and happily for the next six years. As a traveller I achieved some success and can claim to have a fairly intimate acquaintance with the business habits of most of the leading firms of the country in the years from 1895 to 1900. It was, perhaps, while on the road that I first felt the great advantage of being the son of my father. As Mr. Gardiner has explained, my father was himself for many years a commercial traveller in the service of a London firm of furniture makers.

If anything could ever induce me to consent to any form of legislative rule and regulation in commercial matters, I would decree that no one should be permitted to express an opinion upon the conduct of industry, upon employers and employed, upon capital, labour, or any of the questions affecting our industrial life, until he had completed a period of at least twelve months as a traveller on the road.

The commercial traveller is singularly well placed for observing both sides of the question, and is thus able to understand and appreciate that sense of balance which is the essence of the industrial problem. He knows, from his own experience and not from mere hearsay, that there are producers and consumers, for it is his business day by day to listen to, to weigh up, and to balance the contending claims of both these parties. He must represent to his customers the point of view of those who make the article he is endeavouring to sell, and he must spend his evenings in representing to his employers, with speed and accuracy and insight, the opinions, often none too complimentary, of the customers who are to use the goods and services he offers. Left under no misapprehension regarding the essential nature of industry, he realises the folly and irrelevance of most public discussions on these matters.

But there are other things to be learnt on the road. Accessibility, the habit of listening, consideration for others and, most important of all, the art of self-discipline. The commercial traveller does not have to sign on or clock off. He is not under the eye of the foreman; his time is his own, and he can, if he will, waste it. He has indeed many a temptation to do so. It requires a great deal of courage and determination to induce a man, who has already done five or six hours' work, to start out on a mile walk along a country lane in the wet, on the off-chance that another man will be in and may be willing to talk to him. It is so much easier to stay in the hotel and explain that you had called the month before and, having regard to the views which your customer then expressed, you did not think it worth while to risk another call to-day. I solved this difficulty in my case in the following manner. It was my custom to reckon my commission by the hour. I was working a sixty-hour week, and if I earned £3 I would then be earning a shilling an hour. I was impressed with this fact, and I made it my endeavour to earn at least that amount in every hour, determining to increase my hourly rate of pay as rapidly as I could. This so-much-an-hour idea became firmly fixed in my mind and did, I think, enable me to persevere at one of the most difficult of all pursuits—commercial travelling—right through the working hours of the day and thus to make a success of it.

But the real foundations of my position as a business man were laid in December 1899, when Hazell, Watson and Viney, who were then owning and publishing *The Hardware Trade Journal*, decided that they would sell it, and offered it to my father; and here comes in a little personal family history to which Mr. Gardiner has referred, and which I can perhaps emphasise. If my father had acted as I imagine most fathers would have done, he would have bought *The Hardware Trade Journal*, added it to his own business, and reaped for himself the benefit of any profit that might be made, keeping the son, as so many are kept, in a subordinate position, as a salaried manager, to wait, as it were, for dead men's shoes. That is the usual method of procedure. My father, as Mr. Gardiner has shown, was built of different material. Moreover, as the public knows, his interests were not really in business. He used business as a means for providing the small income that he required to enable him to carry on his public work. I was, at the time to which I refer, manager of *The Cabinet Maker*—an unqualified success—and manager of *The House*—an equally unqualified failure, both enterprises being conducted on my father's account.

When the offer of *The Hardware Trade Journal* came our way, Sir John, with a wisdom for which I have reason to be devoutly grateful, saw an opportunity to allow the son to develop on his own account. He therefore offered me the chance of running this new concern, while at the same time allowing me to retain the management of the old. *The Hardware Trade Journal* in those days was a very small affair. It was published monthly, and its total revenues from sales, subscriptions and advertising amounted to some £1,800· a year, sufficient only to cover the production costs and to leave a very small margin.

My father had not much in the way of surplus funds, and I, of course, had very little money. The story of how that part of the problem was solved will be told in a later chapter. But the establishment of *The Hardware Trade Journal* as a business by me at the age of twenty-four marked the end of my period of apprenticeship as a publisher and the beginning of my real life's work.

In this way I was definitely committed to business, and I have never ceased to be sincerely thankful that, in spite of other opportunities and offers, I followed what must have been an inherent inclination.

The business man is born and not made, but he must find that fact out for himself. Business ability would seem to depend on a sense of balance, or is, perhaps, equivalent to a right frame of mind about business things. Some time ago it was thought that Mr. Henry Ford would be a candidate for the Presidency of the United States of America. About that time I had a conversation with a leading American who was an enthusiastic supporter of Ford. I protested that Ford could surely never be President, for the simple reason that he was known to have had no education, that he was, in fact, almost illiterate. The reply was interesting. It reflected in a sort of way much that I am trying to say in this chapter.

Ford an illiterate ! Well ! Thank God for it. See what education has done for the world in developing this abuse of government. Henry Ford possesses from Heaven above *the economic sense* which is something outside education and which, if put into the White House, would make things go, make things balance, sweep away all this sophisticated nonsense of the present time, and you would have no more unemployment, no more want and no more wars.

Thus spoke in characteristic fashion an enthusiastic Yankee with a bee in his bonnet. He was suffering, as I am perhaps suffering, from a keen sense of all that trouble that is brought upon the world by the failure to appreciate the supreme service of the business man, and the absolute necessity for encouraging and developing the qualities which he possesses.

In my view, it is to the business man that we owe almost everything we possess in the material way, and, as I see it, the only hope of securing better conditions or a higher standard of living, not only for the workers, but for the people as a whole, is in the increase and encouragement of a competent class of business men working for the common good on competitive and individualistic lines.

Far too much importance is given by thinkers on industrial questions to the making of things and far too little to exchange and distribution. It can be argued that the making of things is comparatively easy, but that successfully and economically to negotiate the transfer of goods from producer to consumer constitutes the more difficult and more vital part of the complete transaction. Justice has never been done to the all-important share of business as business in the economic scheme of things.

Of the few technical qualifications which are essential to the business man, one is that he must have what may perhaps be described as the book-keeping mind. It is not necessary that a business man should be a book-keeper, but he must understand the principles upon which accounts are kept. He must have the ability to judge a transaction by its effect upon the ledgers. The annual balance-sheet must be always in his mind; which is only another way of saying that he must recognise the essential truth that any work to be successful in this world must bring satisfaction to both buyer and seller—to the consumer as well as to the producer; only thus can a true estimate of worth and expedience be formed. There is much more money lost than is made on estimates. The world is full of people prepared with arguments and figures to prove how profitable this or that transaction should be, and it is the part of the real business man to be such a master of " final figures " as to judge correctly whether these arguments are sound. Most estimates, certainly most public estimates, contain little more than half the expense that will be incurred in connection with an undertaking, and no man can judge such estimates wisely unless he is able to see not only the beginning but the end of the account.

Second in importance to what may be described as the book-keeping mind I would place, as a necessary qualification for a business man, the time sense. The saying is that " time is the essence of the contract." Everyone is familiar with the phrase, but very few really understand it, and a still smaller number act upon it. The most profitable piece of business in existence may be turned into a loss if only sufficient time is taken in carrying it through to completion. If the theory of exchange is properly understood, the necessity of insistence upon the time factor becomes obvious. You cannot afford to spend more time upon a piece of work than the equivalent of the time which the consumer is prepared to give up to the acquisition of whatever benefits he derives from that same piece of work. If you do, the balance is upset, and the work is uneconomic. The money-maker must therefore be a stickler for time. He must work to a time-table and keep himself and everybody else strictly to it. Lack of appreciation of the time factor is one of the most fatal weaknesses of the Labour Movement. The bureaucrat, from the nature of his calling, can know nothing of it; and there is only one lawyer in a thousand who knows what time means. Twenty-five years ago I had the good luck to find such a one.

Business, thoughtfully and economically conducted, carries with it a satisfaction which cannot be surpassed, so far as I am aware, in any other branch of activity. Only those who are in it can realise its complications and its charms. For instance, I buy a load of paper, a simple transaction in which one man undertakes to deliver to me so many tons of material, and I undertake at a given date to pay so much money. That is not business. That is the most elementary introduction to a business transaction. I have then the all-engrossing pleasure, the exhilarating anxiety of devising ways and means of covering both sides of every sheet of paper with something which, when each sheet is folded and transformed into a newspaper, will induce many thousands of my fellow-beings of their own free-will and inclination to put down the money to buy those sheets. That money must then be collected by me from thousands of different sources, must be divided by me among authors, artists, printers, block-makers, and many other newspaper workers, and there should be enough left over to meet my obligations to the paper-maker and provide me with a living.

Doing business is doing real things. Things done in business carry with them a satisfaction which does not always attach to things done in the professions, politics, or other walks of life. In that everybody must be satisfied there is absolute and unqualified freedom on every hand. No one is subjected to any form of pressure or coercion. It is no good trying to impose your ideas upon others. You must secure complete agreement all round. You must devote yourself entirely and whole-heartedly to the task of giving satisfaction to both producers and consumers, between whom you stand, or you cannot continue in business.

And then there is the clean air, the honest atmosphere of commerce; an atmosphere cleaner, brighter, and more honest than any other atmosphere I know. It is almost the only department of human activity in which you can get a really clear issue, in which everything that is done is done for its own sake without ulterior motive. Such singleness of purpose is seldom possible, for example, in politics. The " yes " or " no " of commerce, simple, straight, understandable, and honest, is hard to find in any other walk of life.

I am, however, far from pretending that business is all happiness. The business life, indeed, has perhaps more than its due proportion of disappointment and failure, but disappointment and failure are not incompatible with happiness. In a general way, perhaps, the nearest analogy to the life of the business man is that of the gardener. Both need to be philosophers. The best-laid plans, like the best-worked gardens, do not always yield the desired results. Just as the gardener is at the mercy of the weather, so is the business man at the mercy of the public whim; but I am not at all sure that in either case greater happiness would result if things were different.

There is certainly not so much happiness in business as when I first started. Half such brain power as one possesses is now devoted to scheming rather than to working. Energies that were at one time concentrated whole-heartedly upon the comfort of the customer or consumer are now dissipated in the intricate task of picking one's way through the maze of legislation, regulation, and restriction which twenty-five years of Socialist tendency in government have created.

All the same there is probably as much happiness to be found in business, as great a sense of satisfaction for services rendered, as much joy in accomplishment as is to be discovered in any other walk of life.

A very successful friend of mine told me many years ago that he attributed most of his fortune to his failures. Paradoxical as it may sound, I believe that to be literally true. I learnt more about the publishing business from 1897 to 1901 than I have ever learnt before or since, in connection with a disastrous failure, which was largely responsible for keeping my father on a very modest income.

Having scored a great success as a furniture trade journalist, he became obsessed with the idea that the public were interested in furniture and decoration. He was twenty years before his time. He argued that there were a dozen popular journals devoting themselves to the dressing and decoration of the body and, that being so, there should surely be room for one which would deal exclusively with the dress and decoration of the home. On this theory he started a monthly journal which was called *The House*. It came out with a strong appeal to the women of the country, in the hope of securing their interest in furnishing matters. I was advertisement manager and publisher of the paper. It ran for three or four years, lost a large sum of money, and came to an end. It failed not only because it was before its time, but also, and chiefly, because of our inadequate knowledge concerning the technicalities of catering for the general reader and the machinery to be employed in marketing for the public. But the experience was invaluable to me. Through it I learnt to recognise our limitations, and it has kept me ever since, with one other fatal departure, from any attempt to go outside the class of business which I think I understand—catering as a publisher always for special interests and special trades and particular classes of readers.

Looking back at this distance of time over the road one has travelled I freely confess that I have not achieved the commercial success that might have been mine. I have been diverted, especially in later years, by an absorbing interest in social questions. I am sometimes called an economist, which is a fatal designation for a business man. I have never been able to give the whole of my mind to the single purpose of carrying on my business and making money. When I hear Socialists talk about the " Capitalist System " I am prone to examine my own position, and I am now wasting my time in writing a book about it, all of which is doing no particular good to my business. Like Mr. Baldwin, " I have never yet known a good workman who could talk, and I have never known a good talker who was a good workman." I am not particularly good at work or at talk, but I make the mistake of doing a little of both.

III

EARLY SAVINGS

THE man who thinks that a fortune will result from the saving of coppers and shillings is hugging a delusion, and it would be absurd to pretend that my position can be attributed entirely to the saving habit. It is, however, perfectly true that too much emphasis cannot be laid on the fact that saving is the basis upon which the whole structure rests. I have been a saver all my life, and it is perhaps because the habit was acquired in my earliest years that it has been consistently maintained.

I suppose it is unnecessary to argue with the reader that saving is the first essential to human life. Unless there is saving, life comes to an end. We have only to eat all the potatoes of this year's crop to make quite sure that no potatoes will exist next year. If we consume every egg that is laid, a couple of seasons would be sufficient to eliminate eggs and poultry from the list of things we enjoy. The argument can be carried right through every branch of human activity.

We all depend absolutely for our continued existence upon the fact that some commodities available for consumption are not, in fact, consumed, but are held over, or " saved," for future use. This is the bedrock of the capitalist system. It does not even matter who does the saving; the all-important thing is that the saving should be made. But saving is out of fashion. Having regard to our increased wealth we save less and less, and such elementary dicta as: " Penny wise and pound foolish," and " Look after the pence, and the pounds will take care of themselves," are seldom heard to-day. Still, we all recognise that something in the way of saving is desirable.

One of the most extraordinary of the many peculiarities of these peculiar days is that, as good fathers of families, acting upon our own responsibility in our homes, we are all anxious to some extent to save a little for the benefit of our children. Nevertheless the moment we put on our best clothes and meet together in the parish council, or in any other form of public assembly, we all vote vigorously for the piling up of debt which these children must eventually pay: and I am sadly afraid that future generations, who will see this problem from a different angle, will curse us for that part of the debt bequeathed to them which is not represented by good investments. I cannot, indeed, deny to future generations their denunciations of the War Debt, which for a century they will, of course, be paying. We ourselves are still paying debts incurred in the Napoleonic wars; but, then, we are still afflicted with notions as to the necessity and inevitability of war. When, as is surely coming about, our great-grand-children grow up in a world which has discarded this form of barbarism, which they will fail to understand, and yet find that they have to pay for our indulgence, can it be doubted that they will denounce their great-grandfathers for the terrible consequences of the last twelve years !

I have mentioned that, when I entered the City at a salary of 5s. a week, I saved half of it. Naturally it is impossible that I could have gone on for a couple of years eating a 6d. dinner five days every week and never have spent a penny in any other direction, so I do not doubt that there must have been lapses now and again. But I am quite certain that the bulk of 2s. 6d. a week was safely put away. After a couple of years, when my money was put up to 8s., I gave up the 6d. three-course dinner on the first floor of the " Apple Tree " and went downstairs with the swells, where vegetarian luxuries were served à la carte. I have to confess that the rise in social status cost me dearly, because for a time it broke my habit of saving half my income.

At the age of twenty-four I performed the first serious and important act of saving by taking out a whole-life insurance policy for £1,000, at a cost of £19 10s. a year. There is no finer form of investment, nor is there a surer way of saving, than life insurance, if undertaken with discretion and with proper advice. Thanks to the fact that I had a few pounds in the bank I was able to take out a policy with a premium payable once a year in advance. This is the whole trouble with life insurance. In the case of many young men that I know, the absence of a few pounds in hand to pay the annual premium drives them to other forms of policy with smaller amounts paid at shorter intervals. This is an expensive and costly process which makes insurance much less worth while than on the annual basis.

Long after it was really necessary, from sheer habit I continued this practice of putting away small sums week by week. Thus, at six-and-twenty, when I became engaged to be married, a Post Office account was opened into which I paid 5s. a week with the object of accumulating £25 by the day of our marriage to pay for the honeymoon expenses. The sum of £25 in those days was worth, of course, a good deal more than it is to-day and was a reasonable allowance for such a honeymoon as we contemplated. As a matter of fact, the whole amount was not spent, because I have had the inestimable good fortune to find a partner in life who shares my views in these matters. As the wedding-presents did not include a dinner-service, we cut our honeymoon down to ten days and bought one with the unexpended balance of our funds.

Writing in 1925, having passed through times in which everything has been happening in millions, it is difficult to get one's mind back to the 'nineties, when £25 seemed such a large sum of money, not only to me, but to most people. It is doubtless this habit of thinking in big figures which makes it so hard for most of us to appreciate the importance of little sums of money. There is good reason for thinking that it is responsible for the extraordinarily scant attention given by this generation to such questions as saving. Few of the politicians, for example, who are so ready with theories of how to obtain everything, ever mention this humble method.

The habit is of far-reaching importance and has wider ramifications than are apparent in the mere putting aside of single shillings. The money which is actually saved is not nearly so valuable as the psychological effect which it produces. Saving, like mercy, is twice blessed. There has to be added to the first shilling another one which would be wasted by a person with the spending habit. Natural savers are very few and far between. The average man is by nature prodigal and cannot do things economically. There are some who find it impossible to move from one town to another without a shower of telegrams or a string of taxicabs. These things are usually quite unnecessary and are nearly always the acts of those who can least afford them. It is a strange confession to come from one who is commonly supposed to be so free from financial worry as I am, but the fact is that even at this period of my life I have never acquired the telegram or taxicab habit. I feel that I have so many people shooting telegrams about and rushing in and out of taxis at my expense that I myself cannot afford to use either of these conveniences.

The girl or the youth who is penniless can seldom play a game of tennis without losing a ball—a piece of sheer waste for which it is generally difficult to find the slightest justification or excuse. I give this common illustration to show that there is a great deal more in the saving habit than is generally realised. It leads to a sense of the value of things.

Paradoxical as it may seem, saving in my case does not mean that I have " got any money." I have all my life been saving and all my life been owing. It will be necessary to go into this more complicated question of finance in a later chapter, but I mention it here to dispel the notion that the saving of money means the hoarding of money. In my case, I have merely used the little I have saved as a means to cover the risk of much larger transactions, and I have always owed much money. The point can perhaps be illustrated from an experience through which I am going at the moment of writing. I have just completed arrangements to erect a building at a cost of £150,000. I do not possess £150,000, but, thanks to years of careful saving, I do possess enough to carry the comparatively small margin of risk involved in a £150,000 transaction and am therefore able to borrow or arrange the financing of this building, at the same time technically owning it. This leads to another profound truth which an economist will some day set out scientifically for the benefit of mankind—the truth that there is no such thing as money, that the stuff does not, in fact, exist. Deep down below all the cheques and ledgers and banks and details involved in my £150,000 building transaction is, I think the simple fact that, having, over a number of years, established a character for responsibility in the balancing of things, I have satisfied my fellow-citizens that I am to be trusted to control affairs. Hence all the detailed machinery called finance comes automatically and naturally to my help and service, and I am able to answer for a building the size and importance of which are indicated by the monetary figure of £150,000. But it is the building which exists and not the money, and it comes into being because there is a man who, so bankers and others think, is the proper person to see the business through without undue loss or trouble.

But I must return to my earlier days. My eldest boy was born in 1904, a year after our marriage. At that crucial moment the saving habit again asserted itself and I began anew the practice of accumulating small weekly sums. A Post Office account was opened in my boy's name, and into it my wife and I each paid a shilling every week. We did this for each of our five children, with the result that they will each of them possess a useful little sum on attaining years of discretion.

The reader, I fear, will be tiring of these shillings and half-crowns, which would not appear to have much bearing upon the figure at which my present income is reckoned were it not for other and more important things. These trifling Post Office savings accounts were but the beginning, and I mention them only to make the story complete, to show exactly where and how I began, and to try to convince the reader that there is something in my theory that anyone can make a fortune who really wants to do so. I began, it is true, with very great advantages in being the son of my father—advantages which in many ways cannot be over-estimated—but they did not include any money, and it is with the making of money that this book is concerned.

Such success as I have achieved is to be attributed to the fact that my money has all, or almost all, been invested in my own business. There is no form of investment that can compare for satisfaction or for safety with that made in a business under the investor's own control. Such money is well spent and always has full responsibility behind it. Therefore the business will be, as a rule, well run and free from any of that sense of irresponsibility sometimes associated with the handling of other people's money.

In my early days in business I was dependent upon credit. Those who know what that means will be aware that any money I could save and invest in the business would immediately produce and yield a handsome return. The man using credit in business is paying very highly for it. The difference between prices for supplies at three months net and monthly less $2\frac{1}{2}$ per cent. represents a rate of interest of 15 per cent. per annum. This will sound to the Socialist like usury, but the bulk of that 15 per cent. is not in reality interest at all. By paying cash and taking what is called a cash discount, the buyer is really shifting the risk of his bankruptcy from the shoulders of his creditors to his own and is actually paying to himself the premium to cover that risk. Thus 15 per cent. is not some figure arranged by Capitalists as a price they demand for the use of their money. It is a figure arrived at by a natural process and is really like all interest or discount, the measure of the pressure necessary upon each of us to make us save. But even 15 per cent., excessive as it may appear, does not by any means represent the extent of the profit that can sometimes be made by one's own money in one's own business. Prompt payment means better buying. Suppliers offer the best goods to buyers known to pay promptly, and, when there is not enough to go round the market, the man who asks credit is left out in the cold. I had definite evidence of this natural reaction when there was a shortage of paper during the War. Publishers, on the whole, are not prompt payers. There are plenty of brains in publishing, but there is not too much capital, and paper is for the most part supplied on long credit. Happening to be one who pays promptly, I had a minimum of difficulty throughout the war shortage.

On the other side of the ledger, if you have enough money in your business you will be able to give extended credit to your customers, and, provided you exercise discretion, there is no more remunerative way of utilising savings. Just as you can make money by paying promptly for what you buy, your customers can lose money to you by taking credit terms.

By using half my income over a period of over thirty years to develop business in this and similar ways, I have been able to increase my trade in regular progression. If the reader will do a little figuring, he can work the whole thing out. When I took charge of my father's business, the total turnover from all sources was a matter of £5,000 a year. To-day my business totals approximately £400,000 a year. Not a very big sum in the light of modern business perhaps, but good enough for the work of one man's lifetime. This is a part of my business story worth stressing. Many a young business man may consider that a turnover of £400,000 is something bigger than he can ever hope to secure. Given enterprise, given a trade in which there is room for expansion, and a conservative basis of finance, built upon saving, there are very few business men who could not, in thirty years, put together a yearly turnover such as mine.

It is not so easy to build up as it was, and in my own experience each year has been a little more difficult. My father's business of £5,000 a year was carried on at a profit of more than 20 per cent. He and his brothers were able, in accordance with contemporary practice, to secure for themselves a sufficient income out of a trade of £5,000. The young business man in this position can work it out. Starting with a trade of £5,000 and a profit of £1,000, saving half his profit and re-investing it in his business, turning it over five times a year (which is a good average rate), thus adding £2,500 to the second year's turnover, and going on repeating this process thirty times, representing thirty years, he will see that a turnover of half a million is not so impossible a thing as he imagined.

The calculation, however, is not quite so simple as this. If to that tedious sum I have set him he will add the complication arising from the fact that the rate of profit over the thirty years will steadily diminish, his figure at the end will be something near the figure I have given.

In my own experience, the 20 per cent. profit with which I started has diminished until to-day it is well under 5 per cent. This question of the diminishing rate of profit is a very important one in considering the larger question of the Capitalist System with which political discussion is so much occupied to-day. It is true now, as always, that no big investment can ever produce the rate of return obtainable upon the shilling with which I started. As my business has developed and increased, my rate of profit has shrunk; and as I have been able to invest larger and larger sums from my savings, so those investments have always and steadily become less and less worth while. This is as it should be, for the reason that the simple shilling is a good deal more difficult to save than the bigger sum out of greater wealth. The man with the big bank balance must invest it, and the natural tendency is for his return to be lower than that upon the shilling, where there is no pressure to invest—indeed the pressure is all the other way. It is, from the point of view of economics, fundamentally more important that the shilling should be invested, and therefore the return on the shilling is better than on the bigger sum.

There is an opportunity here for some literary genius, some writer with the ability to grip the imagination of the public, to tell us the story of the shilling a week. The well-being of mankind itself might be woven round this simple little act of saving.

Beginning with the most elementary and obvious fact as it exists to-day, everyone knows, or at least everyone ought to know, that if he will take the trouble to put away a shilling a week for a period of twenty years, he and his successors can for ever afterwards receive an income of 2s. a week. That is the rock upon which Mr. John Wheatley came to grief in the grotesque explanation of the finance of his housing scheme, which will go down to history as the most absurd utterance ever made from the Treasury Bench. It seems on the face of it, and I admit this frankly to the Socialists, a gross injustice that, because some parsimonious person is willing to put a shilling a week into the Post Office Savings Bank on behalf of his infant son, and continues to do so until the son is twenty years old, that favoured boy, through no merit of his own, and having made no effort in the matter, but merely by being the son of his father, should thereafter be able to exact from his fellow-creatures, not only for his own life, but for the lives of all his successors in title, an income of 2s. a week. Yet that is the fact, and a fact which, when we come to work it out, is right, just and proper. It is not a capitalistic scheme to rob the workers of the surplus of their production; it is not a conspiracy of profiteers—it is simply the natural operation of a most natural law.

Let us begin our investigation with a statement which will not, I imagine, be disputed by the most heterodox of modern economists—that saving is essential. It follows that a saving must arise from the willingness of some individual to restrain his desire, to defer some act of consumption, and to wait. The saving which is essential to all of us will thus be seen to depend upon the amount of inducement found to be necessary to make the individual willing to refrain from some form of indulgence.

We will reduce this to the simple terms of a daily experience. As I walk to the station in the morning, I light a pipe of tobacco. I look at my pouch and consider how suitably I am supplied with tobacco, how much I shall need before I return home at night, and this is the sort of mental process through which I go:

"You want some tobacco—No, you don't—You've a couple of pipe-fulls—One after lunch—One on the way home—You're smoking too much, my boy—The doctor says it's not good for you—If you buy a shilling's-worth of tobacco you'll only smoke more and waste a shilling—Put that away and it'll be 2s. in twenty years—Two shillings will be of much more use to your kids than a shilling's-worth of tobacco to you—All right, I'll have my two pipes and wait till to-morrow—I don't know—I've got a lot to do and I may as well be comfortable—This pipe tastes rather nice—Somebody may borrow a pipe-full and then I shan't have one to come home with—What's the good of saving a shilling?—It only means more income tax— And then I'd forgotten, there's that Capital Levy . . ."

By the time I have gone through that argument I

D

am at the station, a tobacco shop is near at hand, and I buy my ounce, and fill up my pipe again.

That is the sort of process that is going on in many different forms in the minds of forty millions of us every day of the week, and it is upon the issue of those millions of little mental struggles that the upward, or the downward, movement of the general standard of living depends.

I have said that the shilling a week put away for twenty years will produce approximately £100, but, for the sake of accuracy and to forestall the meticulous critic, it is as well to point out that the investment will want careful and systematic management to bring about that result. As soon as the shilling has mounted up to a sovereign it should be transferred from the Post Office deposit account and invested in some form of Government Security, where it will begin at once to earn interest nearer 5 per cent. than the $2\frac{1}{2}$ per cent. allowed on deposit. If National Savings Certificates are included in this scheme, the rate of increment will be a little higher, but, in any case, experience shows that the present inducement of 5 per cent. is not sufficient to lead enough of us to make the sacrifice necessary to save for the benefit of all.

Having accumulated the £100 by the wearing process of twenty years of saving, it is possible to invest it at 5 per cent. and secure for ever an income of approximately £5 per annum, or 2s. per week. But this is the smallest return obtainable from this sacrifice. As a matter of fact, it is very easy in these days to invest £100 and get a return of 25 per cent. The advertisement columns of newspapers are full of tempting offers of houses. Thanks to the operations of building societies and other organisations, £100 cash will secure a house, the balance of the purchase-money being paid out of the rent. Assuming the proper rent to be 10s.

a week, it will be seen that the £100 is in fact invested at a rate of interest of 25 per cent., and that at the end of another fourteen or fifteen years that simple 1s. a week may have turned itself into a capital sum of £500, £600, or £700.

This chapter on saving would be much better understood in America, for nearly every street in that country has a savings bank at one corner—a fact which, it may be, explains the absence of that enthusiasm for Trade Unionism and other forms of collective activity which is at present a leading characteristic of our country. It is interesting to speculate on what would have happened if the money contributed over the last twenty years in Trade Union dues had been applied by individuals to the purchase of houses. The melancholy fact is that, had the drive and enthusiasm which two decades ago forced the bulk of the workers to economise so as to support the Unions been put into a great movement to buy their own houses, we should to-day have had 10,000,000 house-owners and no housing problem. That this is not the dreamy conjecture of a person obsessed with the saving idea is demonstrated beyond question by the well-known fact that there are in the United States 11,000,000 working men who own their homes, apart from the 10,000,000 who possess motor-cars and the larger number enjoying such minor advantages as telephones.

Saving may be described as a form of foresight, as the action taken upon thinking always twenty years ahead. The whole science of Capitalism wants bringing down from the lofty phraseology of economists to the solid basis of the shilling-a-week.

Regarding things from an opposite angle, consider the large fortunes made out of the shilling-a-week by the traders who supply on the hire-purchase system. Think of the numbers of armchairs now reposing in the parlours of the workers for which payment is made by this magic shilling-a-week. Here you have the obverse of the Capitalist coin. The essence of saving is that the sacrifice must precede the benefit. Hire purchase is an attempt to put the benefit in front of the sacrifice. Many years ago Mr. Micawber called attention to the vital difference existing between 19s. 6d. and 20s. 6d., and Dickens in that way began the story, which so badly wants developing, of the power and benefit of the shilling-a-week.

Much more might be made of the tremendous advantage which the small investor, very properly and very naturally, has under Capitalism. Illustrations could be given of how small sums can be invested at 100 per cent. Suppose, for instance, that a pair of bad boots cost a sovereign and last six months. The buyer of those boots pays £2 a year to keep himself shod. Then suppose that he has 10s. in hand which he has saved and is therefore in a position to buy better boots at 30s. a pair having a life of twelve months. His annual expenditure on footwear is thus reduced to 30s. and the 10s. is giving him a return of 100 per cent. If that buyer has managed to save rather more and has a five-pound note in hand and is thus able to invest in three pairs of boots, using them in rotation and giving them enough time to recover before he starts out again on a wet day, it will be found that the boots will last almost indefinitely, and his investment will multiply more rapidly. Exactly the same thing is true of most small requirements of life. The poor pay through the nose regularly and systematically, because they have so few shillings in hand to enable them to resist the attractions of cheapness. This fact is generally recognised, but what is not recognised is that there is no remedy except the remedy to be found in individual saving.

This chapter does not pretend to explain the present size of my income, which could never be reached this way, and this way only. My purpose in setting out all these simple and trumpery little matters is to give the reader an insight into the sort of person that I am, and the way I look at things, because therein lies the whole secret. The business man might be described as the great economiser, the great saver. The business classes are nothing but that small section of the community which is doing the saving necessary for the continued existence of the whole. That saving, essential to all of us, brings great advantages to those who make it— and if there is a feeling that those advantages are too great, that the price paid is too high, the remedy is not to destroy the business man—that would merely bring everyone else down with him. The remedy is simple, obvious, and in the hands of each one of us. It is to multiply the number of business men, to develop the business habit, to increase the number of savers. In so far as we succeed in doing this we diminish the benefits which accrue to those who save.

There are various ways of serving one's fellows, but the service rendered by the savers, the business classes, is not recognised at its true value. So far, indeed, from being recognised, the successful business man is held up as an abuse, and that is, to my mind, one of the greatest injustices of these extraordinary times.

WEALTH IS EXCHANGE

IT is to Karl Marx that we owe the popularity of the theory that wealth consists of labour applied to land. From this profit is supposed to accrue, and the notion has been elaborated and developed until the most serious economists now find themselves discussing what is called the " Surplus Product."

The work of Marx was done so well that most people more or less accept the idea that the working man, with his hands, makes a piece of wealth which is then sold at something more than the price charged by the workman, the difference being the surplus, and the distribution of this so-called surplus has formed the theme of many lengthy and weighty volumes. The extraordinarily lop-sided way in which the discussion has developed is perhaps due to the fact that all parties will insist on concentrating their attention upon the position of the wage-earner and limiting the discussion to that issue only.

Mr. Sidney Webb brought the Marxian theory up-to-date some thirty years ago by the historic admission that labour might be done by brain as well as by hand. So we have wealth defined as " land plus labour by hand or brain." But we still continue to argue and debate about the mythical surplus which, under what is called " Capitalism," is supposed in some mysterious way to be filched from its rightful owners—the possessors of " labour power."

If it were true to say that wealth is composed of land and labour, it would be equally true to say that music consists of catgut and horsehair, or that literature is comprised of paper and ink.

John Stuart Mill, whom scarcely anyone reads, owing probably to the fact that he preaches no revolution, defines wealth as " all things useful and agreeable *having exchange value*." That is, in my opinion, the most concise definition of wealth yet enunciated. I would like to simplify the definition still further to the three words with which I have headed this chapter.

Such a definition would not contain the whole of the truth, but it would be a very great deal nearer to the truth than the Marxian formula of land and labour.

I propose to show that exchange is the very essence of wealth, and that land, labour, brains, and many other elements that are found when a close analysis is undertaken are all of small importance compared with this intangible ingredient expressed by the word "exchange."

It does not matter one little bit what may be the system under which we work, what it is called, or how it is devised; nothing can ever alter the fact that if we wish to be civilised we can only live by the will of others, who are willing to give us those things which we require in exchange for something which we have to offer. This rule is of universal application. The journalist who writes may produce stories by the ton, but they will bring him no benefit unless he can persuade other human beings like himself that some advantage will accrue to them from the reading of his stories, and that the advantage is worth some share of their possessions. The doctor who takes a fee of £100 for performing a special operation, which occupies him for thirty minutes, is only able to effect such an exchange because the person upon whom he performs is willing to assess the thirty minutes' effort of the doctor at a value that may represent as much as six months' effort on the part of himself. It is true that some, with greater skill in the arts of exchange, are able to make bargains more profitable to themselves than others, but when it does occur that some detail of this great process of exchange is arranged in such a manner as to bring an undue advantage to one of the parties, the quickest, surest, and most effective remedy for any injustice thereby inflicted is public knowledge, which has never yet failed to bring numerous other men into the same market and so reduce the terms of the extortioner as to bring the transaction rapidly down to a normal and equitable level. If the doctor's £100 is, in the light of public opinion, too high, there will be a widespread desire on the part of young men and women to enter the medical profession. If, on the other hand, it is thought to be an inadequate return for the trouble of learning how to be a doctor, students will be discouraged, and there will be a shortage of doctors. It is all a question of exchange.

There has recently been a correspondence in the newspapers in which it has been argued that, if it is a true statement that wealth is exchange, then there can be no such thing as a profit; the contention being that, if exchange is fair and equitable, neither party benefits at the expense of the other, and neither makes anything that can be called a profit. To be satisfactory such a discussion would have to be founded upon an agreed definition of profit, which might turn out to be nothing but our old friend " saving." If two men exchange an hour's work and one consumes all that he receives while the other saves half of what he gets, do they both make a profit? It is all a question of what is meant by the word. Let a man work by himself on a desert island, and produce day by day rather more than he consumes, thus gradually amassing buildings, implements, and clothing; he will be making a profit just as surely as the merchant who sells an article at a price which leaves him something over and above the actual cost of production. If there be two men on the island who arrange to exchange with one another clothing for buildings, or food for fuel, they each undoubtedly profit from the transactions. If a third man facilitates their operations by conducting the exchange on their behalf and retains for his services a portion of the goods exchanged, he also, like the other two, enjoys a profit. It is an entire misconception to suppose that profit is an illegitimate addition to a price. In a free market, under a system of free competition, nothing is contributed to the general service of the community so cheaply as that essential element known as a profit.

Should any reader feel a doubt as to my definition that " wealth is exchange," or still feel inclined to favour the idea that land and labour are the essence of wealth, I invite him to go through a very simple mental exercise.

If you will select some trifling commodity, some little piece of wealth, and devote your mind for thirty seconds to thinking of it, the process will help you to follow my argument. Take, for instance, the collar that you are wearing, and examine it closely. What is it? How was it made? Where did it come from?

You will find that you bought it in the Strand, London, for a shilling; that it was made in Leicester, with machinery, some of which came from Manchester, some from the United States, and some from Germany; that it is composed of Irish linen manufactured in Belfast from flax grown in Russia. So, within thirty seconds you have travelled round half the world; you have been brought up against the problems of iron, steel, coal, transport, and power, and, most wonderful and complicated of them all, credit banking and finance.

When you pause to consider that in some miraculous way a part of the shilling, which you paid in the Strand for the collar you are wearing, operates to provide the peasant in Russia, who reaped the flax from which the collar is made, with a cup of tea from China or a cigarette from Cuba, you get an elementary insight into the complications of this thing called " wealth," which Karl Marx so glibly argues is brought to our service by the effort of the manual labourer.

Examining more closely this simple little train of circumstances surrounding your own collar, you will notice that unless the peasant in Russia were able to get the cup of tea from China, you would to this day be without your collar; and these considerations should bring you to the conclusion that the girls in Leicester who iron collars might be prepared to iron for generations, that the labourer in Belfast who unloads the flax and loads up the linen might push bales about till Doomsday, but no collar would ever appear upon the scene. Similarly, the peasant in Russia might grow flax till it filled the Universe and still there would be no collar. Land, in this case represented by flax, and labour, represented by hundreds of persons involved in dealing with the odd things that eventually come together in the form of a collar, are the most unimportant details compared with the genius of organisation and foresight which, through the centuries, and thanks to the operations of free exchange, have made it possible for all these agencies to fit into each other and enable you to possess a collar which, incidentally, would take you weeks to make yourself and would then be a very poor collar.

The essential benefits conferred by the operations of exchange are seen also very plainly when we consider the position of the poorest man among us. Were he to devote himself to work for twenty-four hours every day and for seven days of every week, and continue in this way for the whole of the seventy years of his life, he could not of his own effort and with the aid of land (which, of course, means everything that comes out of land) make by himself a tithe even of the trifling things which he possesses. It would take him a week to carve out the piece of bone necessary to make one of the buttons which help to keep his poor rags together. Thanks to the wealth-producing power of exchange, even the poorest of us receives far more than a single individual could ever produce.

Owing to the highly-developed state of our civilisation, this exchange business is becoming so complicated as to be obscured and hidden from the great majority of people. It is, for instance, a little difficult to believe that when I write an article which appears in a Chicago newspaper, I am in fact exchanging my article for a hat which was made at Denton in Lancashire. But that is a fact none the less, and, were it not for this essential thing called " exchange," and the wonderful way in which the machinery of civilisation has perfected it, neither the article nor the hat would exist, and no wealth, in so far as either of them can be described as wealth, would come into being. The man in Denton who makes my hat declines point-blank to read my compositions. The Chicago man, on the other hand, would not be seen dead in the hat which the Denton man makes. But those difficulties—very natural and proper difficulties—are overcome by the system of free exchange, a system under which I am able to find, 5,000 miles away in Chicago, those with the peculiar type of intellect which appreciates my articles, and gain for myself in return a little bit of the produce of Chicago represented, probably, by wheat, which I am able to use in a manner to satisfy the man in Denton, who is thus willing to give me a hat.

Bastiat puts the exchange theory thus, in very simple terms: "Does the farmer make his own clothes? Does the tailor produce the corn he consumes? Does your housekeeper continue to have your bread made at home after she finds that she can buy it cheaper from the baker? Do you resign the pen for the brush to save your paying tribute to the shoeblack? Does the entire economy of society not rest upon the separation of employments, the division of labour—in a word, upon *exchange?* And what is exchange but a calculation which we make with a view to discontinuing direct production in every case in which we find that possible, and in which indirect acquisition enables us to effect a saving in time and effort?" [1]

The business man is the agent of exchange, and, because it is, as a rule, far more difficult to exchange an article than to make it, the business man generally secures a higher remuneration for his part in wealth production than the labourer who performs the simpler and easier work of wielding the hammer or the saw.

One justification for this lies in the fact that exchange involves risk, and the recognition of this element of risk is of primary importance. Let me give an illustration. A man sets to work to make buttons. His object is to earn a living, which is another way of saying that he intends to serve his fellow-creatures by exchanging with them buttons for other commodities. We have already noticed that it would take each one of us several weeks to carve out the pieces of bone forming the buttons upon our clothes. Our button-maker therefore puts down a machine which is calculated to make a million buttons per annum for the next ten years, and he thus begins a process of exchange

[1] *Sophismes Economiques.*

which will not be completed until the ten millionth button is made and stitched on to somebody's shirt ten years hence. But who can say that in ten years' time anybody will be willing to accept and use this particular type of button and put upon it the value which it is calculated to possess at the time when the maker first instals his machinery?

That simple illustration brings out the element of risk in the exchange which takes place between all the individuals concerned in the making of the machine and the man or woman who ten years later gives of his or her goods or services to secure one of those buttons.

A normal piece of exchange often takes ten years, and the services rendered by the persons who take the risk involved in that lapse of time form a very essential part of the process of wealth production. It is not merely lending money for ten years. That is a question of interest and is comparatively simple. The risk factor is quite a different consideration.

On this risk factor hangs the real case for private enterprise. The fact is that a very large proportion of these risks are bad risks. It happens as often as not that at the end of the ten years the button market has changed. The button made by the ten-year-old machine is no longer acceptable, and a loss is incurred. Others cannot be found willing to give of their goods and services in exchange for it. Thus a large proportion of the machinery or apparatus put down for the making and exchanging of things ten years ago is lost and wasted, and the individuals who have carried that risk have lost their money. On the other hand, of course, it sometimes happens that the risk which is carefully calculated for ten years turns out better than was expected, and the owner of the button-making machinery may be reaping advantages for twenty, thirty, or forty years, securing perhaps a return of many hundreds per cent. for the risk he has undertaken.

When all these good and bad risks are put together, it is known that the reward in the aggregate is a modest one. Before the War, capital, as a whole, secured a return of 4 per cent., which represented a mean result of big and little gains and big and little losses.

Here we have a powerful argument against the theory of nationalisation, or State trading, and a strong reason why private enterprise must be the only agency through which we can conserve wealth and secure further progress. If we were citizens of an all-providing State which undertook the manufacture and marketing of our requirements, we should have the right to call upon the State to undertake the risk, either good or bad, involved in carrying out our individual ideas, whether in the making of buttons or the production of newspapers. It could not decline to give to every citizen his right to have his ideas developed. The check on the exploitation of bad risks provided by the possibility of personal loss is the only check which can save us from complete and utter bankruptcy; for, notwithstanding the fact that the rate of indulgence in risky transactions is diminished by the powerful deterrent contained in this fear, we still run risks which involve serious private loss and fail to balance the gains to any appreciable extent, and are only able to save the modest 4 per cent. upon the capital of the people as a whole to provide for further development.

Buying and selling in business is not quite so simple an operation as may be thought by the uninitiated. A newspaper enterprise provides a good illustration of the modern workings of exchange and shows in a striking way how all parties can benefit, even when exchange may appear on the surface to produce a loss. As an example of what really happens I may be allowed to cite one of the weekly trade papers which I publish, *The Cabinet Maker*. A house-furnisher pays me 25*s.* a year to secure fifty-two weekly copies of *The Cabinet Maker*. In return for that 25*s.* I supply him with 50*s.* worth of unprinted paper. The paper which he receives in the form of his weekly organ before any print has been put upon it or any work applied to it has actually cost me 50*s.* The same subscriber will receive in postage stamps upon the wrappers the equivalent of 10*s.* in the course of the year. During the same period I have to pay to printers, photographers, block-makers, artists, and many other people, to say nothing of editors, an average of £3 per subscriber, so that in respect to the house-furnisher who pays me 25*s.* I actually pay considerably more to other people for goods and services which I pass on to my subscriber; no doubt can therefore be entertained as to the benefit which my subscriber derives from this little piece of exchange.

The other half of my business is done with the advertiser, who pays me £10 to have his announcement printed on a page of one week's issue of *The Cabinet Maker*. If that advertiser were to decide, instead of using a page of *The Cabinet Maker*, to make his announcement in his own way through the medium of a circular, he would pay for paper, printing, postage, wrappering and addressing something nearer £25 to reach the same people. There can be little doubt, therefore, that the advertiser derives great benefit from exchange with me in this particular way. Seeing that some thousands of these advertisers think it worth while to pay me £1,200 a day for this kind of service, and that some of them have for over forty years been doing the same thing, and are doing it in increasing quantities, the evidence of my own business would appear to be conclusive that the exchange, as far as the advertiser is concerned, is a satisfactory one.

And yet out of these two apparent losses I make money. My loss to the subscriber is actual, definite, and heavy. The newspaper proprietor does really lose on every reader that he secures. Yet he goes on devising new ways of securing new readers on whom he can lose more money. The loss on the advertiser that I have described is not real, because an actual profit is made by putting together the announcement of a number of advertisers and printing them all at once.

A successful newspaper therefore provides a good example of the way in which exchange brings profit and advantage to all the parties concerned.

The more the exchange, the more the wealth; from which it follows that freedom of exchange is vital to our well-being. The reader who can accept this view of things will be led with me to a deep conviction that not only is Protection, with its international obstructions and obstacles, a destroyer of wealth, but that all obstacles to the free flow of exchange must operate to limit the quantity of wealth available for the use of all. The wealth destroyed nowadays by the activities of trade unions and trade associations is the most distressing and appalling fact in the economic situation. Not a very pleasant reflection for one who professes to believe, as I profess to believe, in organisation and co-operation. The pitiful truth is, however, that we human beings do not seem able to get together for the purpose of doing things. As soon as a dozen of us meet as parish councillors, or as trade union delegates, we proceed at once to make arrangements to prevent things from being done. If trade unions and trade associations were to devote their brain power to speeding up the exchange of goods and services, they would be of enormous benefit to mankind ; but, since they prefer to throw the bulk of their energies into 'the restraint of production and the hindrance of exchange, they are to-day grave dangers to the commonweal, and are robbing the world of untold wealth which it might enjoy.

Exchange must be free if we are to get the best out of it. There must be no force behind it other than the force of individual desire. There can be no satisfactory exchange between the private individual and the bureaucrat, for instance. Each one of us must be quite free to make, or decline, the exchange at his pleasure. Only so can we guarantee that exchange will be fair and equitable, and that there will be benefit on both sides. That is one of the reasons why governments cannot trade. It is the absence of freedom which makes the Post Office, little though people realise it, one of the scandals of the age.

There is probably no remedy in the case of the Post Office, but it is as well that we should recognise what are the true facts, so that we may avoid the error of repeating the waste and loss of our postal arrangements in connection with our mines, railways, or food.

When the free citizen approaches the counter of a Post Office for a 1d. stamp, he is tied hand and foot in the bargain which he contemplates making. He cannot go elsewhere. He cannot compare the value offered with any other. He must give of his wealth exactly what is demanded, if he would have the benefit of a postage stamp.

It always amuses me to hear the Socialists hold up the Post Office as a model of the blessings we should enjoy under State trading, and it is a matter of some surprise to me that so little effort is made to analyse and examine this supposed blessing. The truth is that the service rendered by the Post Office will not stand

E

comparison with the service rendered by private enterprise.

My business as a newspaper proprietor brings this out fairly clearly. In Fleet Street we collect the news of the two hemispheres in a matter of a few hours, put it into readable form, print it, and distribute it over the country; and for a modest penny the individual is provided at his breakfast table with full information of the happenings of the world up to midnight on the previous evening. But if the Fleet Street worker wants to send a letter to his sister in Bedford, he must write it, pay the Postmaster-General 1½d., and put it in the appropriate box at the appropriate Post Office, all before 5.30 p.m. in order to get it to his sister in Bedford half an hour after the story, which is at that time on the telegraph wire from China, has been received, written, composed, printed, packed, distributed, and delivered at the same address in Bedford for two-thirds of the price which the Post Office demands for the mere act of delivering the letter.

The absence of the benefits of free exchange is further brought out when we consider the telephones, in which connection this great country, which once led the world, is quickly becoming the most backward place on earth, for this simple service costs more and more year by year as the Government monopoly grows more and more oppressive.

The appalling fact that the unhappy makers of telephones have recently been obliged to form an association to educate the public in the use of the instrument and overcome public prejudice against bureaucratic incompetence, shows the depths to which we can sink when we neglect the essential principle of exchange.

We have fallen into the habit, by forgetting exchange, of looking upon work as an end in itself instead of as a means to an end. We think of a job as something we want for ourselves, forgetting that its only excuse is to supply the needs of others. If all of us who are employed would ask ourselves the question: " Are we giving good value; are we making fair exchange; are we creating in the breast of the consumer a feeling of satisfaction, a desire for more; are we rendering good service ? " and if we would allow this spirit to govern our work, we should not only be assured of the security of our own employment, but be creating employment for others.

When a woman enters a shop and puts down a shilling, taking away an article, if she says to herself: " This is a satisfactory transaction; I am very pleased with what I have got; I think this is a good shillings-worth," she tells others about it, she comes back for more as soon as she can, and thus trade is promoted, exchange is developed, business is good, and employment plentiful.

If, on the other hand, when she puts down her shilling and takes away her article, saying to herself: " What a swindle! What a frightful price! I call that a ' have,' " she goes away with the determination to do without any more of that article as long as she can; to try to make it herself (as she is now doing in thousands with her gloves), and trade is bad, exchange is discouraged, and unemployment rife.

Reverting once more to my definition, a possible amplification of it might read: " Wealth is exchange; money is the medium of exchange."

Money was invented by merchants to facilitate exchange. It is therefore the medium of exchange and nothing else. Exchange started as barter, when somebody bargained a sheep for a sack of corn. In the course of time, through the process of experiment with various forms of tally, money as we know it was evolved. The man who bargained his sheep for a bag of corn, because he wanted corn, had all the trouble of finding not only another man with corn, but a man who, having corn, also wanted a sheep. Through the medium of money we have complicated and simplified things to the point of perfection which is reached when I can use the services of the reader in Chicago to satisfy the man who makes my hat in Lancashire.

But it is important to remember that money is nothing else than the medium of exchange. The attempt to use money for purposes other than exchange is responsible for a very large share of the troubles from which the world is suffering. The worst of poison or of sin is that, as a rule, so much of either is necessary to make its nature obvious. Drink, in small quantities, is, or some people think so, a pleasant and agreeable thing. But drink taken in large quantities is a very dangerous form of poison. Gambling, similarly, can be to some people harmless and amusing. But if we did nothing else but gamble, there would be an end of money and of wealth. In the same way the sin of using money for purposes other than exchange can be committed in small and minor ways without doing any more damage than does an occasional whisky and soda or an occasional shilling a hundred on a game of bridge. When we begin to make a habit of using money without regard to its natural and essential purpose—exchange—we are doing exactly the same as if we took to drink or gave ourselves up to gambling, and are as surely steering for calamity as in the other cases we should be for delirium tremens or bankruptcy.

Money rightly used is a measure or token of some article or some service which is exchanged for some other article or service, the exchange being calculated by the parties to be equitable and proper, and thus represented on both sides by a given amount of money. When Mr. Lloyd George goes to the Paris Peace

Conference, and writes down thousands of millions of marks or francs or pounds; which never existed, and never will exist, and never can bear any relation to exchange; which have no backing in the form of real things; he is using money for a purpose which is foreign to its nature. He fails utterly to accomplish his object, and he dispenses widespread damage and destruction to money and all that it means to the rest of us.

Nothing shows more clearly the crying need for a far closer attention than is usual among us to the science of economics than the acceptance as a right and proper thing, in these later years, of the haphazard handling of money by our politicians. It is very difficult to get the public to think seriously of these questions. The voter is concerned about his own few hundreds a year, and his mind it would seem declines to function if only the politician will talk of enough millions. The fact is that when we depart from the principle of exchange, money ceases to function. This same argument requires development in other ways. There is no exchange about a dole. There is no exchange about an old age pension. These things are, like drink, only possible in moderation. There is bad exchange when we talk of " ninepence for fourpence." Again, there is no exchange when a mechanic declines to work unless his labourer is sitting, smoking a cigarette, at his elbow. These abuses arise from the growth of the notion that we can, through political action, alter economic law. The misapplied effort of Trade Unionism in the last twenty-five years has doubled wages, and, in the main, no one is much better off. The rise of the standard of living in the last generation has been slower than in any other generation since the industrial revolution. The first three-quarters of the nineteenth century showed progress at a rate unprecedented in the history of man, progress always increasing. The last quarter of that century and the first of our own have, it is true, shown a certain progress, but the rate goes steadily down. The miraculous benefit of electricity, for instance, had it been used with the same freedom and energy as was steam, might have lifted the standard of comfort high above that which exists to-day, but it has been largely wasted by this modern habit of pursuing money for its own sake and forgetting that it is merely the medium of exchange.

Money, like electricity, must be generated before it can function in any way. Like the electric current, it lies dormant, giving no sign of its existence, until the dynamo, to which the business man is analogous, is set in motion. The activities of the dynamo liberate it from its invisible and inexhaustible sources, the brushes of commerce collect it from the commutators of exchange and distribute it over the wires of public circulation to perform the multifarious duties of the civilised world.

Thus I argue that wealth is exchange, that there is no real surplus in connection with exchange; that if the market were free we should be exchanging that which we possess in the way of power of muscle or brain for similar qualities possessed by others, and that the only surplus or profit that does exist arises from the fact that here and there some of us are prepared to conserve some portion of that which we produce, thus through " profit " creating capital, and pave the way for further exchange and further production.

THE STORY OF THE " H. T. J."

The Hardware Trade Journal, affectionately known to its intimates as the " *H. T. J.*," was established in 1874 as the circular of a big Midland factoring house of those days, Martineau and Smith. It was, when I took it over, a small monthly with an annual gross revenue of £1,800. It is now, in 1925, one of the big trade weeklies of the world, with gross revenues of some £70,000 per annum. It does not pretend to rank as literature; it knows nothing of politics, poems, or the picturesque, but it deals with cooking-stoves, drain-pipes, mouse-traps, and the mass of commonplace articles which, although our comfort and happiness depend completely upon them, are not ordinarily mentioned in Acts of Parliament, in fiction, or even in the newspapers.

Trade, so far as the ordinary writer is concerned, is still understood as indicating iron, coal, cotton, and ships. We have yet to learn as a people that the trade upon which we depend consists of all the various odd-ments that are in everyday use. The iron trade, for instance, provides us with nothing but the raw material upon which an infinite amount of work has to be per-formed before any of us in the ordinary way come into contact with it at all.

The big raw material trades, by virtue of their size and comparative simplicity, assume an exaggerated importance in our system of economy. In reality we are much more dependent upon kettles, pen-knives, and brace-buttons than upon ingots; and the majority of the trade, employment, and work involved in bringing iron to our service is performed after it has ceased to interest the iron trade and the orthodox political economist.

Were it not for the avowed purpose of this book, some apology would be necessary for inflicting upon the reader a detailed story of my early connection with *The Hardware Trade Journal*. As will appear, it has nothing about it which could not be found in the early story of most business enterprises, and to the experienced business man it may seem dull. I publish it because I hold that it is the clear duty of the business community to undertake the education of the public in the science of business. We have clung far too long to the old tradition that business should not be discussed out of business hours, forgetting the fact that some twenty-two million electors are now the real controllers of affairs in business. And since politicians are determined to occupy their minds with our affairs it seems to me the paramount duty of my class to teach them something about the details of a business undertaking, and thus help them to take decisions which have a measure of knowledge and fact behind them. Here, then, is the story of the " *H. T. J.*"

In December, 1899, Mr. F. J. Francis, who had been working for twenty years previously in a sub-editorial capacity on *The Ironmonger*, secured an option to purchase from Hazell, Watson and Viney *The Hardware Trade Journal*, which was then a monthly. Mr. Francis, an energetic and progressive middle-aged man, was actuated no doubt by the desire to exercise full authority as editor, a position that did not appear likely to be available on *The Ironmonger*. At that time I was secretary to Benn Brothers, Ltd., and advertisement manager of *The Cabinet Maker*, and no doubt, like Francis, I felt the restraint of superiors and seniors who did not appear too anxious to make room at the top. Thus, when Francis and I came together, there was a combination of personal force and ambition, which is the first essential to success.

Francis, in the first place, approached my father. I was not then, in the business sense, worth approaching, but my father handed him over to me, and, with the consent of my old firm, I was allowed to develop the new business, while retaining the position of secretary and manager of the old.

I had very little money—Francis had still less; we could not, by ourselves, take advantage of this offer to sell by Hazell, Watson and Viney. We thereupon prepared and issued the prospectus of a company called the Hardware Trade Journal, Ltd. In that prospectus, we explained the wonderful scheme we had devised for financing and running a trade journal. We hoped to secure the requisite capital from the retail ironmongery trade, the idea being that the trade would be willing to invest in a newspaper whose mission it was solely to voice its views. The scheme was an early and very crude edition of the plan now being operated by Mr. J. St. Loe Strachey with *The Spectator*. In our case it was thoroughly bad, because it introduced a number of unsound financial considerations.

The ironmongers who bought from advertisers in the journal were to receive preferential dividends according to the amounts of their purchases. In this and other ways, which appealed very strongly to the inexperienced minds of Francis and myself, the scheme was quite unsound.

We gave the company a nominal capital of £7,000 in 7,000 shares and issued the prospectus broadcast to the ironmongery trade. Hazell, Watson and Viney, then, as now, one of the soundest concerns in the country, guided by some of the shrewdest and kindest heads I have ever met, treated the young company promoters with caution, but with a generous helpfulness which will always remain in my mind as the first of many experiences in direct contradiction to much that I hear from pulpits and platforms, and most that I read in literature, of the grasping hardness inseparable from association with commerce. They thought well enough of the scheme to accept the purchase price of £1,500 in shares, coupling that acceptance with the condition that I should enter into an undertaking to buy the shares over a period, I think, of seven years. In this connection, the life insurance that I had effected a year or two before came in useful as collateral security. I give this part of the story in some detail as it illustrates rather well much that I shall have to say on the question of risk.

It cannot be too much emphasised that in the conduct of any industrial or commercial undertaking risk is the vital element. Here was a great firm owning a nice little property and selling it for £1,500 with a risk. In return for their risk, they secured, firstly, a chance of getting a good price for their property, and, secondly, an order to print a journal. They took the risk that a young man of twenty-four, with some claim to know something about the business, might be able to earn enough money at it to pay them £1,500 over a period of years. The arrangement was one that suited me admirably. It was good business on the part of Hazell, Watson and Viney, and in the end it has turned out well for both of us. The chances in 1899, however, were at least even, that Hazell, Watson and Viney might lose their money and that I might become bankrupt.

The next bad thing about a bad prospectus was the provision that it made with regard to myself. I was to be managing-director, and the prospectus set out in a flowery, separate paragraph how I, with all my experience in trade paper publishing, had been good enough to consent to serve the company in return for shares instead of cash. Shares to the number of 2,500 were thus allotted to me and I was bound to act as managing-director without further remuneration for five years. Francis entered into a similar arrangement; though, in his case, he only compounded part of his salary for shares.

The prospectus was then issued, and it produced practically no response. I remember that by return of post an Irish ironmonger sent in an application for one £1 share, somebody else asked for five, and I do not think that at the end of a week £100 had been subscribed. The two promoters were in despair. There appeared to be no hope whatever. The scheme must fall through. At that stage I had a heart-to-heart talk with my father, who appeared to be very little surprised that the trade had not rushed to secure the advantage of this glowing prospectus. He was not in any case very much enamoured of prospectuses and companies with outside shareholders, but he recognised that in the circumstances in which we were placed some steps had to be taken to secure some working capital. Though he could ill afford it, my father offered to subscribe 500 shares if we could find some members of the trade with sufficient confidence in the prospects of the journal to take up at least an equal amount.

Francis, who, by reason of his long connection with *The Ironmonger*, was known to the leading men of the industry, rushed round the country and, by strong personal pressure, scraped together 1,000 shares.

It will be noticed that this company was formed before

the Companies Act of 1908. Had the formalities since imposed upon company promoters been in force at the time, they would have killed our enterprise at birth.

In March, 1900, we produced our first issue of *The Hardware Trade Journal*, having at the back of us £1,500 in cash capital and my undertaking to pay £1,500 to Hazell, Watson and Viney for the shares which they held in the company. This was my first big debt.

As soon as I had acquired the copyrights, I made up my mind that I would publish weekly, as I have always held that in periodical work of this nature seven days is the limit to the interval that should be allowed to elapse between successive issues.

The years from 1900 to 1907 were, without any question, the hardest years of my life. The first three of them were spent in association with Mr. Francis, he as editor and I as publisher and manager; but when he died, his end being unquestionably hastened by the strain of that period, I became both editor and manager of the paper. I called myself managing-director because it sounded well, but it simply meant that I managed myself and four or five juniors. That was the extent of the staff that the paper could afford. I did for a time the whole of the provincial travelling, wearily searching the by-ways of Birmingham, Glasgow, Sheffield, and Manchester for makers of hardware goods willing to advertise them in the pages of the " *H. T. J.* "

The story of the early years can, perhaps, best be told in figures. I have the accounts back to 1903, but for the first two years I must rely upon my memory. By March, 1901, when our first balance-sheet was struck we had lost rather more than £900. By March, 1902, our second balance-sheet showed a further loss of some £200. The next year showed a profit. The following are the subsequent figures down to the year before the war :

Year.			Profit. £	Year.			Profit. £
1903	...	...	95	1909	...	...	1,442
1904	...	...	403	1910	...	...	2,308
1905	...	...	570	1911	...	...	2,875
1906	...	...	606	1912	...	...	2,209
1907	...	...	935	1913	...	...	2,538
1908	...	...	1,612				

I am a firm believer in prompt figures, and have always declined to work in the dark. On April 10th, 1900, I had completed a profit and loss account for the month of March, and on or about the 10th of every month, for each of the 300 months that I have traded since then, I have had exact figures showing the previous month's transactions and results. The expansion of my business has depended entirely upon these prompt figures. I have been able all along to know exactly where I was and exactly what I could do. I have thus never lost any time when there was the least justification for progress or expansion.

As soon as I could see a profit I have always used it, and when my position was not such as to justify anything but caution I have known it.

Nor have I been content to rely solely upon figures of business accomplished. The profit and loss account for the previous month does enable one to know exactly where one stands in relation to one's debtors and creditors, but it does not always constitute a sure guide as to what is likely to happen in succeeding months. For this reason I make a habit of keeping a separate set of accounts indicating, in a more or less rough way, what are the prospects of the immediate future. The newspaper business lends itself fairly readily to this system of forecasting, because, with subscriptions paid in advance and advertisements secured for periods ahead, it is possible to gauge with fair accuracy the income and expenditure of the future.

It will be seen from the figures given above that my financial position in the first few years of *The Hardware Trade Journal* was, to put it mildly, precarious. The £1,500 cash capital with which I started was barely sufficient to cover the difference between the debtors and creditors of the business. The first use of capital is, of course, to enable one to pay wages for months in advance, before the retailing of the finished article brings any income into the business. At the end of the first year I had lost £900, thus making the position extremely difficult, and it was then that I first took to the practice of accepting bills.

Bills of exchange are at once the most dangerous and the most beneficial of all the devices of finance. They can develop a despotic tyranny as well as a friendly subservience. Personally, though for years past I have discontinued their use, I still look back upon the bill of exchange with feelings of affection.

For the benefit of the uninitiated, a bill of exchange is a document in which one man declares that so many days after its date he will pay to another man a given sum. The form of words usually used is, for example, " London, March 10th, 1900. Four months after date pay to our order the sum of one hundred and twenty-five pounds two shillings and sixpence for value received." In the left-hand bottom corner: " To Mr. E. J. P. Benn, 11 Finsbury Square, London, E.C.," and in the right-hand bottom corner: " Thomas Printer & Co." Across this document, written by the acceptor: " Accepted, payable London and South-Western Bank, Finsbury Branch, E. J. P. Benn."

The very essence of the good bill of exchange is contained in its last three words, " for value received," for if these words are true, the bill is a perfectly sound form of currency. The bill has, it will be seen, three parties associated with it. The first is the drawer, the second the acceptor, and thirdly, if he will take a hand in it, the banker.

The drawer, having got the bill accepted, takes it to his banker to discount, and the banker will, as a rule, give the customer the present value, that is to say, the amount stated on the bill, less the discount according to the bank rate of the moment. In discounting a trading bill the banker has the double security of the acceptor and the drawer. When the bill falls due he presents it for payment at the acceptor's bank, and if then it should be dishonoured he returns it to the drawer—his customer—debiting his account with its value. The banker thus lends money to—say—Thomas Printer & Co. on the strength of the joint credit of Printer and myself.

It will be noticed that in 1901, when I began accepting bills, I had not very much credit. My banker would give me a good character in respect of the small amount of business that had passed through my bank account, but he would not have been willing on the strength of my figures to recommend me for credit to the amount that I was then in debt. So I was thrown back, as every young man starting in business with insufficient capital must be thrown back, upon the generosity and judgment of other business men; or rather, strictly speaking, I relied for my continued commercial existence upon that class of idle rich about whom so much nonsense is talked by politicians and others.

Reviewing the transactions of those days in the light of a much fuller knowledge of economic matters than I then possessed, one sees again the inner functioning of exchange. Idle rich possessors of money had risked their capital in sundry businesses such as paper merchants' and printers', and that capital was now used to finance me. The true nature of the transaction was obscured behind contracts for paper and printing, but the fact remains as stated. The idle rich, in the guise of shareholders and proprietors of paper and printing houses, were willing to take the risk of allowing me to buy printing and paper on long-credit terms, the prices, of course, being adjusted to cover the risk involved.

However much one may criticise their position, these persons rendered to me and, as I claim, to the community a real service, and I have never yet been able to doubt the indispensability of such service to the common well-being and to the economic safety of the whole.

Having lost £900 in the first year's trading, the balance-sheet of the Hardware Trade Journal, Ltd., was distinctly uninviting, and, it will be remembered, it was encumbered with an item of 2,500 shares held by me in respect of five years' services to be given to the company. The position was so serious that it was obviously necessary to do something in the way of writing down. I therefore consented—I confess with some reluctance—to surrender my shares and allow them to be cancelled. It may be imagined what a wrench this meant to me in the position in which I then was. A year before I had suddenly blossomed forth as a capitalist, the possessor of a handsome share certificate testifying that I was the owner of 2,500 shares of £1 each. To be robbed of this tribute to my business status at the end of a twelvemonth was not at all agreeable. But it was the only thing to be done. My concern must be as near to solvent as possible; my accounts must be ready for examination when more credit was wanted, and so I surrendered my shares.

In place of them I made an arrangement which shows

the confidence I had in the undertaking. It offered, it is true, very little immediate return, but it has since produced three-quarters of my income. I made an agreement with the company whereby I was to receive the sum of £300 a year, and, in addition, a quarter of the profits remaining after a dividend of 10 per cent. had been paid upon the shares issued. The shareholders were content because it gave them some prospect of a dividend. They were sure of a 10 per cent. return before the man who was working the concern secured anything worth having for himself.

Another year passed to 1902, when a further £200 had been lost and the position was apparently worse. By this time, £1,100 out of the original £1,500 working capital had gone completely. This meant that our liabilities must not be more than £400 in excess of our assets, an impossible position which was negotiated by the intervention of the bill of exchange.

At this stage of the proceedings things to the outsider looked fairly hopeless. They were not, however, so hopeless to me. I had endured two years of hard struggle with the advertisers and subscribers whom I had secured, or hoped to secure, and I felt that things were moving in the right direction; but it was hardly to be expected that shareholders would take the same view. At the end of the second year one of my shareholders with a hundred shares was tired of the transaction, having received no return upon his money, and suggested to me that I should buy him out. I had nothing much with which to buy out him or anyone else; but by that time my credit was improving. I had by then accepted and paid quite a number of bills of exchange and bankers were getting more accustomed to my signature on these documents. I had no bad mark against me at the bank of any of my customers, and at my own bank, when a cheque was drawn or a

F

bill matured, sufficient money was always there to meet it, so that I had, notwithstanding all the difficulties of these two years, acquired a certain amount of that indefinable but essential thing known as credit.

I was therefore able to buy my shareholder's 100 shares, giving him in respect of them four bills of £25 each, payable at three, six, nine, and twelve months. The shareholder took some risk in transferring the shares to me on these terms, but his view then was, and he was probably quite right, that the bills appeared to be a little more valuable than the shares, upon which no prospect of return had yet appeared.

By degrees, the knowledge of this transaction spread to the rest of my shareholders. With a unanimity for which I have never ceased to be thankful, they one and all approached me in the hope that I would treat them in the same way. In the course of three or four years, therefore, I had bought the whole of the shares that had been issued originally on the prospectus, except my father's 500 and Hazell, Watson and Viney's 1,500. I was then making some little progress, but chiefly in the direction of extending my credit. My bill-book was my chief concern. Every few weeks some payment to a shareholder, a printer, or a paper merchant would be due, and every few weeks some new creditor had to be found. The process was thoroughly sound and good with a serious person, as I undoubtedly was, and with a serious business, as I undoubtedly had.

Reduced to simple terms, my regularly recurring problem was how to pay £100, finding somebody of whom to borrow £90 of it and using £10 of my small savings to meet the remainder. In this way, although my total commitments were constantly mounting, my assets were mounting at an even higher rate, and the difference on the right side was getting always a little greater.

The man who owns a sovereign and owes 25s. is bankrupt. But the man who possesses £5,000 and owes £4,500 is solvent enough, if only he can persuade his creditors to wait for their payments until he can conveniently realise his assets. That was my position.

About this time—my records are to-day missing, but I think it must have been in 1903—I paid off Hazell, Watson and Viney in the same way on bills. Looking back, I think I must have been a bold person in those early years, cheerfully accepting loss and responsibility from which I fear I should shrink to-day. For by 1903 I had acquired on credit £2,500 of shares, I had assumed responsibility for big debts for paper and printing, I had purchased a small rival paper called *Ironmongery* from Messrs. W. H. & L. Collingridge, also on bills, and on January 3rd, 1903, I was married.

Naturally there were times when this financial part of my work produced serious difficulties. There would be periods, particularly in the autumn, when money was tight and customers' accounts came in very slowly; and, now and again, but not often, really complicated obligations had to be undertaken. I found on one occasion a jobbing printer so anxious to have our orders for circulars, stationery, and sundry printing that I used him to help me out of a difficulty. I transferred to him for £200 in cash a couple of hundred of the bigger mass of shares which I had taken upon my shoulders, he undertaking to sell them back to me as soon as I could manage to buy them, and I undertaking in the meantime to give him a few hundred pounds' worth of work. The work was, no doubt, expensively paid for, but, still, it had to be done.

It will be noticed that in this way I had acquired

complete responsibility for the business and become the owner of practically the whole of the shares of the Hardware Trade Journal, Ltd.

By the time the company had turned the corner and was making profits, those profits were for the most part mine. After the first few years they began to be worth having, and a reference to my table on page 77 will show how, by the end of 1908, I was quit of bills of exchange and accommodation creditors.

A word must be said of the kindness, consideration, and helpfulness with which I was met all along the line by the many business persons with whom I came into touch during these strenuous and to me, eventful years.   Only once do I remember any attempt really to take advantage of me, or to play the money-lender. I was received by the majority of those whose business it is to supply the requirements of the publisher with consideration, with sympathy, and with sound judgment.   I paid the proper price for my paper and my printing and my credit.   The prices were, of course, more than I should have had to pay had I been able to offer cash, but the extra price was not more than was necessary to cover the risk involved in giving me credit. A year or two ago, in pursuance of my public work, I was taken seriously to task for expressing the opinion that there was more of the real spirit of Christianity to be found in business circles than in many churches, and I offer the story of my own experience as some justification for a view which I still hold.

It must not be assumed, however, that *The Hardware Trade Journal* was received by its prospective customers with open arms. The task of finding advertisers and subscribers to support it was extraordinarily difficult. Advertisers in particular were less than reasonable. I was offering, and I can say so now with the fullest sense of responsibility, good value for money, and I might have been supported far more freely than I was. But the attitude of the market as I found it, and as I believe it generally to be to any new proposition, especially of this class, was: " It sounds all right; it may be good; go on, see what you can do with others. If you don't die in the attempt and are alive in three or four years' time, we may begin to look at you."

This is the hard side of private enterprise. But it is that hardness which makes it sound and equitable. The market has to be very sure that you believe in your own article before it will accept it. I went into a free market without the ability to impose my ideas upon anybody but myself; where every buyer and every seller enjoyed perfect freedom to accept or reject every proposition made, and I had, quite rightly and properly, to satisfy the market that the article I was trying to sell was good enough for them to accept by the evidence of my own willingness to stand or fall by it. I gave that proof, and thus the market was sure that my service was worth having.

It is in this part of the story that I should acknowledge the good fortune that has fallen to me in the shape of colleagues on my staff of exceptional ability and untiring energy. I have been able by degrees to build up a most accomplished body of industrial publicists, and thus have reached the present position when every week nearly £1,500 comes into and goes out of the coffers of *The Hardware Trade Journal*. Every penny piece of this large sum is freely paid in and freely paid out, without a suspicion of compulsion or obligation in any way on either side. This great journal now stands as a perfectly balanced part of the trade of the country without exacting any cost from anyone, without making any call or demand upon a single individual or a single sovereign that does not participate freely and willingly.

It will be obvious that in the early years, and ever since, the spirit behind *The Hardware Trade Journal* has been the forward spirit. It has never mattered very much what would be the effect of some particular action at the moment of its doing. The all-important point has been, what would be the ultimate effect? This forward-looking policy is essential to the successful conduct of a newspaper business. Our whole interest is not so much the size of the profit on the individual transaction as the continuity of that profit; from which it follows that we always work on the smallest margin that we can possibly accept, in the hope that it may be a continuous source of income.

The life of every business is, of course, absolutely dependent upon the satisfaction given to its customer. There is nothing to be gained by making a few sovereigns out of an advertiser this week, if that advertiser is not going to secure satisfaction and remain a customer for the thousands of weeks to come, when the journal will still require advertisements.

In the long and trying process of creating confidence and finding favour with the market, it has been necessary to indulge in what are now known as " stunts." The trade paper in 1900 was, on the whole, a poor affair, consisting mainly of trade notices. I have written hundreds of puff paragraphs for manufacturers, having no other object in view than to flatter them in the hope that they would advertise.

" Messrs. Jones and Brown, the well-known firm of Sheffield manufacturers, whose celebrated edge-tools have secured for themselves a world-wide reputation, not only for quality of material and excellence of workmanship, but also for a combination of reliability and economy altogether above the average, have issued a new spring list . . . " etc.

That sort of thing is still written, and it is to my credit that quite early in my publishing life I cut it out. The trade Press is now practically free from this abuse, and the daily Press is almost the only place where the manufacturer, in consideration of his taking space, can secure a " puff " paragraph informing the world of his personal qualities as well as his goods. I may be permitted to find some amusement in the fact that the popular and the daily Press have in recent years adopted a method long ago discarded by their trade and technical contemporaries.

We ran for a time a comic page, and we did it extremely well. I spent more money than I could afford employing Tom Browne, then the foremost humorous artist of the day, to produce, once a month, a page of funny sketches for the amusement of the hardware trade. That funny page, no doubt, helped a little, but it taught me that humour, though a useful addition, cannot be regarded as a sales-promoting agent. Advertisers are now discovering that the funny advertisement defeats its own object.

Another " stunt " which I ran is much more interesting in these later days. I was for a time actively employed in a movement which was known as " price maintenance." Strange as it may seem to us, who are struggling with a class of retail tradesmen clinging too long to inflated profits, the trouble in the early part of the century was to get the shopkeeper to make any profit at all. In his desire to render the greatest possible service to his clients his weakness was to cut the price of an article to a point at which it was worth nobody's while to touch it. Finally, in self-defence, manufacturers initiated the movement of price maintenance, whereby the makers of a special line attempted to force merchants and retailers to preserve a fixed price in the selling of those articles. I may further claim that, as a young and struggling journalist, I did a very daring thing in this connection. A big firm of drapers in the provinces, known as price-cutters, bought quantities of well-known hardware lines, branded goods that had been well advertised, and offered them to the public at prices less than the actual wholesale figures. These drapers, on the principle of throwing a sprat to catch a mackerel, were actually selling hardware goods at less than cost price to attract custom for their drapery wares.

I sought out a drapery expert and induced him to visit the various establishments of this great drapery firm and make a number of purchases of smaller lines, not so well-known to the public and upon which the margin of profit or loss was not so obvious. My expert came back with a bunch of receipted bills and a bag full of drapery sundries: half a yard of veiling; a yard of delaine; a boy's shirt; a pair of braces; a pair of corsets; and, I think, some shoes. On each of these articles the drapers in question had made a profit which varied from 200 per cent., in the case of the corsets, to something over 700 per cent., in the case of the veiling. I published a series of articles explaining how these people were persuading the public that they were real agents of economy, when, as a matter of fact, at the expense of my hardware manufacturers, they were securing exorbitant profits upon most of their own merchandise. It brought me very near to a lawsuit, but we made the most of it. We published double-column advertisements in the local newspapers, offering to subscribe £200 to the hospitals if our statements should prove unfounded.

Another case occurred a year later, when I convicted one of my biggest advertisers of similar practices. Here I took a stronger line. I published my charges in the form of innuendo, and secured from the firm a cate-

gorical denial and angry threats of actions and damages.
Not until the discussion had reached this stage did I
produce my evidence in the form of receipted bills and
names and addresses. That case cost me a good customer, and lost me an advertising revenue I could ill
afford, but it was good journalism, good service to the
trade, and I have never regretted it.

As a result of my experiences in connection with *The
Hardware Trade Journal* I hold very strong views on
the theory of competition. To my mind it is established beyond question that competition, so far from
being a curse and a danger, is the highest form of
economic blessing. In 1900, when I began with *The
Hardware Trade Journal*, one of the foremost trade
papers in the land, if not in the world, was *The Ironmonger*, then, and now, published by the old and
respected firm of Morgan Bros. I was out, frankly,
to beat *The Ironmonger*. Day by day, with subscriber
after subscriber and advertiser after advertiser, I was
engaged in argument as to the respective merits of the
two papers. The competition through the twenty-five
years I have been concerned in it has been definite and
serious. It is, of course, true that if some subscriber
decides to read one paper, and one paper only, he must
take either *The Ironmonger* or *The Hardware Trade
Journal*, and that in taking the one he will appear to
be robbing the other of a reader. The same argument
holds good of the advertiser.

But with over twenty years' experience behind us, and
full figures to go upon, the fallacy of the argument
against competition is demonstrated almost to perfection. On page 90 are the figures of the pages of advertisements published by the two journals at the beginning
and the end of twenty years. The number of pages of
advertisements is a rough but fairly accurate gauge of
the position of a newspaper and the size of its business.

Pages of Advertisements Published

—	1901	1920	Increase per cent.
The Ironmonger	5,344	10,824	100
The Hardware Trade Journal ...	971	7,850	800
Total	6,315	18,674	—

The result of my twenty years' competition with *The Ironmonger*, in so far as I have had any effect on it at all, has been to double its business. In the meantime I have multiplied my own business by 800 per cent. The market in ironmongery journalism, so far as it can be gauged from advertising, has grown from 6,315 pages to 18,674 pages. The amount of money involved (and here, of course, I have to calculate roughly, because I have, naturally, no access to the ledgers of my competitor) was in 1901 somewhere in the neighbourhood of £35,000, and in 1920 approximately £180,000.

It must be assumed that this money which is spent annually in the pages of *The Ironmonger* and *The Hardware Trade Journal* is, on the whole, well spent, and that it is therefore a sum which represents a very much larger amount of business which results from all this advertising. The hardware trade puts down £180,000 for the purpose of assisting the sale of its goods, and if, for the sake of argument, we assume that the trade as a whole allows in its cost accounts 5 per cent. for advertising, then there was transacted, as a result of the advertising of 1901, £700,000 worth of hardware sales. On the same basis the amount of business for which *The Ironmonger* and *The Hardware Trade Journal* can claim responsibility in 1920 was £3,600,000.

So that, following this very speculative argument to

its logical conclusion, the most obvious result of my twenty years' competition with *The Ironmonger* in the promotion of hardware advertising has been to add £2,900,000 to the turnover or trade of the hardware industry as a whole.

This figure is probably a very gross under-estimate of the trade that has actually resulted from all this effort. It can be checked in another way. *The Hardware Trade Journal* in the first six months of 1924 instituted a competition in which it invited retail ironmongers to keep a record of their purchases from advertisers and others. and, as the prizes amounted to £1,000 in cash, a good many records were kept, and the figures produced were representative and reliable.

Out of this competition there arose a discussion as to the value of the retail hardware trade of the country, and the argument narrowed itself down to a point where it was agreed on all sides that the retail ironmongers of the land were doing a business of not less than £80,000,000 per annum—probably a good deal more. From this it may be argued that in claiming £3,600,000 worth of trade as a result of the efforts of the hardware Press, I am, in all probability, seriously under-estimating its value.

These figures have some interest in connection with current political discussion. That the little ironmongers' shops all over the country, never mentioned in political controversy, forgotten by the Communists, left out of account by those who are so busy putting the world right, should be doing a trade of £80,000,000 a year helps to explain the deep-seated scorn and contempt with which the business classes regard futile arguments over such things as Russian trade agreements and the paltry few millions that are held up as vital to the general well-being.

It is not difficult to imagine what figures such as I

have quoted mean when translated into terms of wages
and employment. I have the satisfaction of knowing
that out of the bank account of *The Hardware Trade
Journal* alone, some £40,000 a year is paid in wages to
the people who are directly engaged in its production,
and another sum almost equal in amount goes to swell
the wages fund through more indirect channels. The
paper carries half a dozen salaries, each of them far
bigger than the whole of the profits of a few years ago,
and is able to pay wages to compositors and manual
workers at rates three times as high as those of 1900.

Those early struggles associated with the establishment of *The Hardware Trade Journal* are in every way
typical of all business growing-pains. There are many
thousands of young men who ought to be encouraged
by every means in our power to undertake the same
kind of struggle. There were in 1900, and there are
to-day, enough real difficulties with customers and
creditors and business technicalities to make the task
sufficiently formidable and to make the number who
will essay it dangerously small. Therefore it seems to
me to be the height of folly that we, as a community,
should make work of this kind doubly difficult by
creating restrictions and barriers in every direction,
either by labour regulations or by legislative enact-
ments. It cannot be denied that the problem which
I tackled in 1900 was easy compared with similar
problems to-day. If I had had to waste all the time in
1900 that I now waste in filling up forms, I am quite
convinced that I should have given up. There were
periods, constantly recurring, when one was forced
seriously to consider one's position, and when every
bit of courage that one possessed had to be screwed
up to the highest pitch. Often very little was needed
to bring the whole effort to an end.

It is too little realised that the business of the country

depends upon a constant supply of new men and new enterprises to make good the deterioration and wastage of the old, and to add that new mass of service which must be available year after year if the standard of living is to rise. That supply of new men is being dammed up at the source by the modern theory that the State machinery can take the place of individual effort.

PROFIT AND LOSS

THE first and by far the most important function of profit is to balance loss. Every business, however successful, keeps what is known as a " profit-and-loss account," and the profit which emerges at the end of a year's trading is never anything but the balance between profits that have been made on some sections of the business and losses that have been incurred on others. In calculations with regard to profits, therefore, it is necessary to bear in mind that there are losses to be set against them. The income tax figures, the dividend figures, the reserves, the bonuses, and all the other items that are used by those who argue about profits, are all wrong if they fail to take into consideration this matter of loss. The tax-collector, for instance, makes no assessment upon the man who loses money, and to add together all the income tax assessments and talk of them as profits in the bulk is to look upon one side only of the account, from which no accurate conclusions can be drawn.

" . . . the number of those who succeed in business," says Professor Marshall, " is but a small percentage of the whole; and in their hands are concentrated the fortunes of others several times as numerous as themselves who have made savings of their own, or who have inherited the savings of others and lost them all, together with the fruits of their own efforts, in unsuccessful business. In order, therefore, to find the average profits of a trade, we must not divide the aggregate profits made in it by the number of those who are reaping them, nor even by that number added to the number who have failed; but from the aggregate profits of the successful we must subtract the aggregate losses of those who have failed and, perhaps, disappeared from the trade; and we must then divide the remainder by the sum of the numbers of those who have succeeded and those who have failed. It is probable that the true gross earnings of management, that is, the excess of profits over interest, is not on the average more than a half, and in some risky trades not more than a tenth part, of what it appears to be to persons who form their estimate of the profitableness of a trade by observation only of those who have secured its prizes." (*Principles of Economics*.)

It is not even possible to divide business men into those who make profits and those who make losses. All of them make both. The most successful man may make the heaviest losses and, because of his success, be able to bear them. The most unsuccessful may make big profits on occasions and, because of the number and size of his losses, they will be of little use to him.

In my own case, I have at one time or another owned or controlled twenty-five newspapers. Of these, sixteen have lost money, and there remain nine successes. I am probably more fortunate than most, and my proportion of nine profits to sixteen losses would, in all probability, be found to be above the average.

The one big argument for the leaving of profits in the hands of private individuals is that losses must also be left in private hands. The problem, considered as a whole, is how to secure that there shall be more profits than losses. Notwithstanding the immense power of the whole mass of private interests, struggling with all the force that they possess to avoid loss, loss is always running a neck and neck race with profit, which has never yet been known to win by more than a short head.

Those who desire to supersede private enterprise would do well to leave for a moment the fascinating discussion as to what they would do with these profits and gains when they had brought them under public ownership, and devote their thoughts to a much more difficult problem, the discovery of some device whereby losses could either be avoided, or shared out, in place of the stupendous individual effort which is now directed to that all-important end.

The next introductory point that should be mentioned in the discussion of profits is the extraordinary fuss that is made about them. Generally speaking, the average standard of most things is low, and the public mind is no exception to this rule; jumping to careless conclusions on insufficient data, it magnifies and exaggerates profit out of all proportion to other and more important considerations in the economic structure. Suppose, for instance, that by a stroke of genius and daring I were to succeed in producing bread at a penny a quartern loaf. To begin with I should put everybody else in the bread business into bankruptcy. That operation would receive no public notice. The public does not get excited about bankruptcies. Next, I should double the supply of bread and abolish hunger. That also would excite no comment. Within a year the whole human race would have completely forgotten that such a thing as hunger ever existed. Not a word of thanks, not a word of appreciation, would come my way. Bread in plenty and to spare would in a twinkling be the right of every citizen. All these benefits would be overlooked, and every one would seize upon my profit. Articles would be written, meetings would be held, policies would be framed, upon the horrible fact that I was a wealthy man. If, in the ordinary course of making and marketing bread, it became necessary, owing to a rise in railway rates, to raise the price by a farthing, the world would howl at the " greed of the Bread Trust," and never a whisper would be heard of the 6*d.* which was the price before I started my operations. That is, in fact, exactly what happened with Rockefeller. His millions are as a drop in the ocean compared with the wealth that he has showered upon every cottage in the world in the shape of cheap light and heat.

The diseased condition of the public mind on this question is in no way better illustrated than by our views on Russia in 1925. Half the world is willing to witness, if not with approval, with silence which gives consent, the reduction of the Russian crops by half, the death by starvation of large numbers of the Russian people, and all the dangerous antics of the Russian bureaucracy, because, whatever else the Bolsheviks may have done, they have made a bold attack upon this evil thing known as profit.

Profit, if separated into its constituent elements, consists of three parts: (1) the earnings of management; (2) the interest of capital; and (3) an insurance premium for the risk undertaken. I have never yet heard a word of criticism or objection levelled at any one of these three essentials to our economic existence when considered separately. Every one agrees that management must be paid; nobody doubts that capital must earn interest; and it is not questioned that some margin must be allowed to cover the cost of risk. But as soon as these three elements are put together and called profits, we are told that we must produce " for use and not for profit "; that we shall never reach the ideal until we abolish the profit-making habit. These

G

critics should surely be rather more specific and tell us to which of the three parts of profit they most object, and which they would first abolish.

Profits are, in the main, as small as it is possible to make them. The largest profits, those which are reported in the newspapers, are, as a rule, infinitesimal when considered in the only way in which a profit should be considered—as a percentage on price. The most superficial examination will show that this must be so. The first object of the serious business man is to make and keep a customer, to build up a trade, and it is an object which he can only achieve if he will give to the customer the maximum of satisfaction. If a shopkeeper can ensure a regular order by accepting a price which represents a very narrow margin of recurring profit, he is infinitely better off than if he has to be searching always for a new customer out of whom he can squeeze an unreasonable profit, well knowing that in doing so he is closing another account. The old adage, "small profits and quick returns," is as true to-day as ever it was and remains a guiding principle for every earnest trader. Profits, therefore, from their nature, will always be, in a free market, calculated on the lowest scale consistent with safety.

The publishing business is more speculative than most forms of manufacturing. There are, no doubt, others equally risky, but, as a publisher, I may be permitted to entertain the notion that I run rather more risk than is usual. The manufacturer of furniture who makes a number of chairs and fails to sell them at once may be in difficulties, but he has at least the chairs with which to console himself. The manufacturer of overcoats who finds, when his goods are ready for the market, that they will not sell, because the fashions have changed, can at worst cut them up and turn them into caps or some other garment that will. But the manufacturer of a newspaper must sell his whole out-put the moment it is produced. If it is not so sold the loss is absolute and complete. It is quite impossible to turn a copy of *The Daily Telegraph* into an Ethel M. Dell novel, or to sell any quantity of last Saturday's issue in the following week. The outstanding characteristic of the publishing business is, therefore, that the publisher must pay the whole expense of producing his maximum output whether he sells it or not, and that, in so far as he does not sell it, he is faced with complete and irretrievable loss. Another point about publishing, which is to some extent connected with the above, is that costs of production bear very little relation to selling prices. This will be made more clear by some of the figures which follow, but it is obvious that in arranging for the payment of £1,000 to some correspondent to explore the position in China or to make a flight across the desert, the newspaper proprietor cannot add that figure to the price of his paper and announce that on Monday, Wednesday, and Friday next *The Daily Telegraph,* on account of special features, will be charged at *6d.* The newspaper proprietor, who is, of course, just as much a manufacturer as is a maker of bootlaces, has to consider the expenses of his enterprise as a whole and his revenues as a whole, and endeavour to make them balance.

I ought, perhaps, to apologise to the general reader for inflicting upon him a series of figures which would appear to possess a minimum of ordinary interest, but the task which I have set myself in writing this book makes it essential. I thereforep ublish on pages 100 and 101 three specimens of actual newspaper accounts. I do not ask the reader to waste much time over them. Figures can never mean very much except to those who have an intimate knowledge of all the circumstances out of which they come. But politicians and

Weeks Ending	Oct. 4th, 1924. £ s. d.	Oct. 11th, 1924. £ s. d.	Oct. 18th, 1924. £ s. d.	Oct. 25th, 1924. £ s. d.	Nov. 1st, 1924. £ s. d.	Nov. 8th, 1924. £ s. d.
REVENUE:						
Advertisements	892 0 10	673 14 6	812 3 7	827 2 4	810 15 4	626 0 10
Sales and Subscriptions	47 0 3	64 17 10	53 12 8	46 0 0	38 1 6	35 15 1
	£939 1 1	£738 12 4	£865 16 3	£873 2 4	£848 16 10	£661 15 11
EXPENDITURE:						
Printing and Paper	529 4 7	414 0 4	436 4 0	475 15 7	442 1 5	400 16 9
Blocks	10 9 7	16 12 11	13 12 8	11 5 5	10 12 11	10 3 5
Contributions	14 17 3	23 19 4	12 8 10	17 19 7	17 3 6	12 2 3
Commissions	9 9 9	11 4 6	11 12 5	14 9 0	13 3 0	9 15 5
Salaries	68 10 6	69 17 3	68 12 3	70 12 9	68 10 6	71 0 9
Trade Expenses	12 10 0	12 10 0	18 10 0	18 10 0	18 10 0	18 10 0
Petty Cash	10 0 0	10 0 0	10 0 0	10 0 0	10 0 0	10 0 0
Legal Expenses	2 5 0	3 5 0	5 5 0	5 5 0	5 5 0	5 5 0
Bad Debts and Discounts	14 15 0	4 15 0	14 15 0	14 15 0	19 15 0	19 15 0
Carriage	1 6 0	1 8 0	1 3 0	1 1 3	1 1 7	1 1 7
Interest on Capital at 5 per cent.	8 0 0	8 0 0	8 0 0	8 0 0	8 0 0	8 0 0
	£681 7 8	£575 12 4	£600 3 2	£647 15 4	£614 8 4	£566 15 7
Revenue	939 1 1	738 12 4	865 16 3	873 2 4	848 16 10	661 15 11
Expenditure	681 7 8	575 12 4	600 3 2	647 15 4	614 8 4	566 15 7
Profit	£257 13 5	£163 0 0	£265 13 1	£225 7 0	£234 8 6	£95 0 4

	£	s.	d.	£	s.	d.	£	s.	d.	£	s.	d.	£	s.	d.	£	s.	d.
REVENUE:																		
Advertisements	127	7	0	209	3	3	157	11	6	173	15	3	200	0	3	161	15	0
Sales and Subscriptions	57	14	8	63	8	1	70	15	6	76	12	9	122	3	6	95	10	2
	£185	1	8	£272	11	4	£228	7	0	£250	8	0	£322	3	9	£257	5	2
EXPENDITURE:																		
Printing and Paper	398	19	4	505	3	6	409	19	8	423	9	3	584	17	5	489	19	9
Travelling Expenses and Commissions	147	18	2	152	4	7	157	1	3	165	5	7	173	2	1	175	18	2
Contributions	46	4	9	49	5	7	45	19	5	45	15	3	44	8	9	45	4	7
Salaries, Postages and Sundries	41	0	0	41	0	0	41	0	0	41	0	0	42	0	0	42	10	0
Trade Expenses, Blocks, Stationery, etc.	35	18	5	58	16	10	37	10	0	69	11	6	39	11	2	34	15	6
Bad Debts and Discounts	3	0	0	3	0	0	3	0	0	3	0	0	3	0	0	3	0	0
Interest on Capital at 5 per cent.	4	0	0	4	0	0	4	0	0	4	0	0	4	0	0	4	0	0
	£677	0	8	£813	10	6	£698	10	4	£752	1	7	£890	19	5	£795	8	0
Expenditure	677	0	8	813	10	6	698	10	4	752	1	7	890	19	5	795	8	0
Revenue	185	1	8	272	11	4	228	7	0	250	8	0	322	3	9	257	5	2
Loss	£491	19	0	£540	19	2	£470	3	4	£501	13	7	£568	15	8	£538	2	10

bureaucrats and committees love figures, and the best way to make them understand how little they can ever know is to supply them with more and more figures. I begin, on page 100, with the trading accounts for six weeks of a very prosperous trade paper.

This is a paper with which I was at one time connected and is a rare case of a valuable advertising medium involving very small expenses and producing very large profits. These profits arise from the fact that the industry with which the paper is connected discovered that it suits its purpose to make full use of the advertisment pages, although the circulation is small and the editorial expenses almost negligible.

On page 101 is given a similar set of figures of an unsuccessful trade paper which came into my hands a few years ago.

Here it will be noticed that the losses are even bigger than the profits in the previous case. This was a paper that had enjoyed a successful career for twenty or thirty years before Lord Northcliffe began his net sales campaign. The paper then came into the hands of an energetic young man, full of theories and good intentions and confident of his complete knowledge of the principles and practice of publishing. He decided that he could beat Lord Northcliffe at his own game and launched a big circulation campaign. How far he succeeded may be judged from the figures which appear in the account.

My third illustration (page 103) is put in a more regular form. The earlier examples are weekly returns such as are produced for the benefit of the newspaper proprietor. These figures show the profit and loss account for a period of eight months of another trade paper. This, again, is an old-established and well-known journal which in its time prospered greatly.

Profit and Loss Account, March 1st to October 31st

	£	s.	d.;		£	s.	d.
To Printing and Paper; ...	3,341	2	3	By Advertisements... ...	2,732	19	8
Illustrations and Blocks ; ...	329	6	5	Subscriptions and Sales...	1,832	10	5
Contributions	170	13	10	*Balance*—NET LOSS ...	1,947	14	7
Postages	215	19	6				
Salaries	1,078	0	0				
Advertising	17	8	6				
Wages	469	19	3				
Rent, etc.	137	6	8				
Rates	28	8	3				
Gas and Electric Light ...	22	0	10				
Telephone	22	1	3				
Printing and Stationery ...	60	3	6				
Insurance	3	3	11				
Bank Charges and Sundry Expenses	81	19	5				
Auditor's Fee	17	6	8				
Bank Interest	16	5	6				
Loan Interest	130	16	3				
Legal Expenses	9	18	6				
Commission	361	4	2				
	£6,513	4	8		£6,513	4	8

My diagnosis of the disease which killed it is excessive economy. It came under management very different from that of the young man who tried to imitate Northcliffe, management whose one idea of business wisdom was summed up in the word "economy." True economy, especially in newspaper work, consists of knowing how and when to spend money. The cutting out of expenses may be a most fallacious policy. This paper, under the blight of parsimony, managed to hold its own until the War came, and with it the increase in printers' charges. The loss of nearly £2,000 is accounted for to some extent by the increase in the printers' account. It is only one of many hundreds of cases of minor publishing efforts driven off the market by the policy that has guided the printing industry for the last ten years. The figures bring out one or two other points that are worth making in passing. It will be noticed that the block-makers took, in the eight months under review, almost twice as much money out of this little enterprise as did the men and women who wrote for it. Contributions amounted to £170 as against £329 for illustrations and blocks, another example of the price we are paying for the organisation of labour into trade unions, and, still more, of employers into trade associations. The business of photo-engraving has been so completely organised and so misdirected that masters and men together have been able to raise their prices to four times the pre-War figure, with results sufficiently obvious in this case. Similarly, the Postmaster-General took from this business nearly half as much as all the weekly clerical wages spent upon it. That is to say, that for every £1 paid to the office staff, clerks, typists, and messengers, the postman, whose work was to carry the finished product to the subscriber, cost 10s.—a further instance of what organised or trustified or nationalised industry can do.

I have already given in another chapter the figures of *The Hardware Trade Journal*. It was one of my successes, and I now add a couple of my failures. In these cases I am able to give the names of the papers involved, because I am completely responsible for each one of the three, and, unlike the accounts to which I have just referred, I have not to consider the interests of other individuals.

In the following table of losses, month by month, incurred during its life by the weekly journal, *Ways and Means*, we have an illustration of the folly of attempting to mix up propaganda with business. This is the fundamental trouble with *The Daily Herald*. *Ways and Means*, a journal of commerce and economics, was published by me during 1919 and 1920 with an object very similar to that of this book. I was foolish enough to imagine that the public might be interested in economic problems looked at from a business point of view. For two years, week by week, I devoted myself to this effort. A section of the public responded bravely. It was willing, Friday by Friday, to pay 6d for a paper that cost 2*s.* or 3*s.* We are thoroughly spoiled in this matter of periodical literature. The Press is really a present to the public from the advertisers. It is obviously impossible to ask people to pay half-a-crown for a two-and-sixpenny journal. They have never done anything of the kind. *Ways and Means* had to be offered for 6*d.* in the vain hope that the advertiser might be willing to make up the 2*s.* loss. But the advertiser knows better. He will support only a paper published to supply the public with what it demands. That is, after all, a logical attitude for him to adopt. The newspaper or journal existing to educate the public makes no appeal to him. *Ways and Means* therefore had to come to an end.

" Ways and Means " Losses

—				1919			1920		
				£	*s.*	*d.*	£	*s.*	*d.*
January	...	...	...	20	10	2	328	13	10
February	...	...	...	173	7	3	252	12	2
March	...	...	...	324	13	11	235	9	8
April	...	...	...	644	9	10	145	8	7
May	...	...	...	625	6	8	341	8	10
June	...	...	...	343	13	11	299	15	2
July	...	...	...	278	17	3	377	7	0
August	...	...	...	160	5	11	577	14	2
September	...	...	...	267	3	1	413	14	6
October	...	...	...	139	10	3	556	18	0
November	...	...	...	347	2	0	416	9	6
December	...	...	...	572	8	4	—		

My last example is of another kind. It serves to bring out the many-sided nature of this difficult question of profit and loss in newspaper and publishing work.

I give the figures from October, 1920, to November, 1922, of a weekly called *Farm and Home*, owned and published by me during that period. This was a good little paper, as is shown by the fact that at one time no less than 40,000 people thought it worth buying. That is not a big circulation for a farming paper, but *Farm and Home* served its purpose in that its matter and policy appealed to small farmers who found in it something they were willing to pay for and to read. On a 40,000 circulation, there is a definite limit to the charges that can be made to advertisers, but the paper from about 1880 to 1920 managed to balance its accounts and produce a satisfactory income for its proprietors. I made two mistakes in acquiring *Farm and Home*. In the first place, like the young man with the ideas about circulation mentioned above, I was vain enough to think that I could do rather better with it than its previous somewhat old-fashioned owners, and that, with those up-to-date methods I am supposed to understand, circulation and advertisements might both be improved and a great paper developed. I proved wrong in these calculations. *Farm and Home* had lived, so it proved, upon its Victorian character. The people who read it did so because they preferred old-fashioned to modern ideas. My proprietorship was unwelcome to them. In the second place, I overlooked (and I confess I should have known better) the question of printers' charges. The paper was one of those which managed nicely on pre-War figures. It was, however, incapable of expansion, and the figures in the printers' bill, four times the size of those before the War, turned a small profit into a heavy loss, with the result that publication had to cease.

" Farm and Home " Losses

	1920			1921			1922		
	£	s.	d.	£	s.	d.	£	s.	d.
January	—			152	10	8	99	15	4
February	—			24	3	3	51	8	0
March	—			46	13	3	117	2	1
April	—			169	8	1	44	5	3
May	—			470	16	10	74	7	5
June	—			1,140	1	10	9	16	9
July	—			502	14	8	347	6	9
August ...	—			168	2	5	59	0	11
September ...	—			412	9	9	26	12	10
October	41	12	9	109	2	7	86	16	11
November ...	97	4	1	95	17	11	58	5	7
December ...	421	7	4	171	4	2	—		

The manufacture and publication of a book presents a problem differing in many ways from that connected with the publication of a newspaper. Two examples are sufficient to make this clear. In October, 1924, I had written and put into type a pamphlet which I called *Prosperity and Politics*, with the sub-title: " The Business Implications of Socialism." When the General Election was precipitated in the middle of that month, it was thought advisable to rush this pamphlet on to the market, and it was given the unhappy title, " Why Not to Vote Labour." We had then to consider what would be the probable sale of the pamphlet; how many we should print; at what price it should be marketed. Two thousand copies could be produced at a total cost of 9*d.* a copy. Ten thousand copies, on the other hand, were quoted at figures which worked out at 6*d.* a copy. The figure 9*d.* would have involved a selling price to the public of 1*s.* 6*d.*, and 6*d.* a selling price of 1*s.* It should be explained that the selling or published price is subject to a reduction of one-third to the bookseller or newsagent. A selling price of 1s. 6d. would therefore produce to the publisher a net return of 1s., and a selling price of 1s. a net return of 8d. If, therefore, we had printed 2,000 copies at a cost of 9d. and sold them all at 1s. apiece, there would have been a profit of £25. If, on the other hand, we had produced an edition of 10,000 at 6d. and sold them all at 8d., there would have been a profit of £83 6s. 8d. It is, of course, impossible in considering the problem of a book at this early stage to gauge with any exactitude how many copies it is wise to print or how many may be sold. Publishing is in this respect like producing a play. Even the greatest experts have never been able to judge beforehand whether a play would run for a week, or whether it would last, like " Charley's Aunt," for years. We might have printed 10,000 copies of our pamphlet at 6d., spent £250, sold 1,500 at 8d., received £50, and involved ourselves in a loss of £200. On the other hand, we might have printed 2,000 copies, costing £75, and sold 1,500 at 1s., exactly balancing the account and leaving ourselves with 500 copies as waste-paper. At the moment of writing, this transaction is not complete, and exact figures are not available, but, on the present showing, I expect to be faced with a loss of £100 on this little speculation.

I now turn to a good book, good not only as a book but as a piece of business, a weighty, technical work, typical of the kind of thing for which my firm has a reputation. The book is in its third year. It was published at the end of 1922, one thousand copies being produced at a cost of £1 4s. per copy. The published price of the book is £2 8s., and the net return to us from the wholesale book trade £1 16s.

The figures for 1923 and 1924, taken at the nearest hundreds, are as follows:

First Year

	£			£
1,000 copies at £1 4s. ...	1,200	Sell 400 at £1 16s. ...		720
Profit	240	Stock 600 at £1 4s. ...		720
	£1,440			£1,440

Second Year

	£			£
Stock	720	Sell 50 at £1 16s. ...		90
Profit	30	Stock 550 at £1 4s. ...		660
	£750			£750

For the purpose of our accounts we have made on this book up to date a profit of £270, and we hold stock valued at £660. The book is selling at the rate of fifty copies a year, and we have enough in stock to supply the market for eleven years to come. If the book holds good for that time and sells right out, I shall make a handsome profit. If, as of course happens with technical literature, this book should be superseded by a better, or the matter which it contains should require revision, or for any of a number of other reasons the demand should fall off, we may be left with our stock. If that should happen, a fact which I cannot possibly know until another five or six years have elapsed, I shall have to write off £660 of the stock as lost. Instead of having made £270, I shall be £390 out of pocket. Meanwhile, I have paid income tax at 4s. 6d. in the £ on the £270, and, if the rate of tax goes down to, say, 2s. 6d., I shall recover taxation at the lower rate on the loss which I cannot discover for some years to come.

The account as set out above requires adjustment in

several minor ways, notably in the matter of deprecia-
tion. Present purposes would not, however, be served
by indulging in complications, and the simple figures
given illustrate, as accurately and conveniently as possible, the complicated nature of this thing called profit,
about which so many wax eloquent, and the distribution and taxation of which appear to the public so easy
and obvious a matter.

Profits are made not only by people like publishers,
who undertake the work and responsibility of organising production, but by others who, being mere owners
of money, invest it in various ways and live upon the
interest or dividends. "The money-owner strides in
front," says Karl Marx, and the impression that one
gets from the trend of political discussion is that
nothing is easier than to live a life of luxury and batten
on the efforts of others. The real justification for the
idle rich lies in the fact that none of us would save, if
we had not a hope of ourselves becoming some day,
and to some extent, independent, and we should all
die if we did not save.

Personally I have never been able to generate for
myself the indignation which is so widely spread at
this abuse of riches and idleness, the reason being that
I have tried to imitate the methods of these people and
have made a ghastly failure of it. Such little money
as I have made has for the most part been invested in
my own business. But out of respect for the theory
that it is not wise to have all one's eggs in one basket,
I have from time to time made outside investments.
I possess not a large but a fair amount in stocks, shares,
and bonds bought on the market after the manner of
the idle rich, in the hope that I might enjoy an income
from the interest arising out of my investments. I do
not like to confess that I am a fool in money matters.
In fact, the evidence would appear to show that I have

been fairly successful in managing money. It is, nevertheless, true that 5s. of every sovereign invested outside my own business has been lost. I am not a gambler; I have not taken undue risks. Whenever I have had a few hundred pounds to invest I have sought advice and considered the matter carefully, but it remains true that these outside investments would realise to-day only three-quarters of what I paid for them.

My opinion is that the much-talked-of idle rich are very largely engaged in losing money made for them by previous generations, who became rich because they were not idle. I have had one or two real gambles. I once backed a clever little man who made out a case which seemed to me unanswerable for making a fortune out of soap. He had a process which he claimed would produce soap in half the time now required for the purpose. Time being the most expensive thing there is, it appeared to me that the idea was good. This little man certainly made soap, and he certainly saved time. It was very good soap, but he overlooked the fact that while he was saving time he was wasting glycerine, which ran away at such a rate that all the time and all the money that he and I could put together were not sufficient compensation for it.

I lost a few hundred pounds over another old friend who had solved the problem of making jam. I went into this scheme revelling in imaginary delights of a world full of jam, and the fortunes that would be showered upon me when the object was achieved. I have also dropped money on clocks. All of which makes me perhaps a little more appreciative than the man in the street of the skill and wisdom of the makers and suppliers of these useful and necessary goods, and a little more convinced that the only people who are likely to suffer from the investing activities of the idle rich are the idle rich themselves.

There is one sum of £100 which I have tried and failed to lose, and of which I am very proud. I put it aside some years ago to carry out an experiment of my own. It has been lent without security on three occasions. First it was lent to an old school friend, one of those decent fellows with middle-class ideas and modest ambitions, whose chief desire was a quiet life. He had the notion that he would settle down in a small country hotel where he could keep a pony, and perhaps do a little shooting. He bought the hotel with my £100 and £200 of his own, and a year or two later, much to my surprise, the money came back. It was next lent to an energetic mechanic whose skill at his trade had frequently attracted my attention. He was a fidgety, ambitious type, altogether different from my country publican friend. I lent him my £100. He began in a small way on his own account, and the sum came back to me with interest within a couple of years. The money next went into the hands of a commercial traveller who wished to run a small agency business of his own and be in a position to give a little credit. Again the £100 came back to me safely, and is now performing a fourth and similar mission.

Returning, however, to my main question, there are much weightier reasons why the factors of profit and loss must always remain in a successful industrial system, and why they should always be left in private hands. Commerce and industry consist in exchange; we all live by exchanging our goods and services for the goods and services of others. The profit or loss is the test by which the mutual benefits of the operation of exchange may be judged. If your goods are acceptable, or your services useful, you will receive a profit. If, on the other hand, your fellow-creatures decide (wisely or unwisely, it makes no matter) that they do not want your goods, or that they will get on better without your services, then you will make a loss. The profit-making system is the only one under which the consumer can be perfectly sure of obtaining the article he wants—any other scheme can only mean that he will have forced upon him the article which somebody else thinks he ought to want.

Working for a profit on an individualistic system also ensures that the people who receive the goods are the same as those who pay for them—a very important point. Based upon the interests of the consumer, it is the only system under which the consumer can ever stand a chance. We can make no money, we can do no good, unless we can persuade others to accept our services at the value that we and they jointly place upon them.

We are asked to work up our indignation over the question of incentive. We are told that the ideal man would " produce for use and not for profit." We are asked to believe that the desire for profit is a base instinct; that it demoralises; that it is not worthy. This argument always leaves me cold for two reasons. First of all, however much a man may want to make money, however depraved may be his liking for money, he is, under the profit system, altogether powerless to get hold of a sixpenny-piece until he is willing to render some acceptable service to others at the price they will willingly pay for it.

Secondly, considering only the welfare of society as a whole, the important thing is that goods should be made and sold; that employment should be found and amenities provided; that the maximum of activity should be maintained, and, if these blessings are secured, it is altogether immaterial what may be the motive or incentive of the man who makes them possible. Every time that he initiates a business transaction he does two things. First, he tends to raise the

H

rate of wages by adding to the demand for labour, and, secondly, he tends to reduce prices to the consumer, by adding to the available supply of commodities. These two direct effects of his operation are so important, so necessary, so entirely beneficial, as to render a discussion of his motives not only irrelevant but unwise. Whatever his motives, he cannot succeed unless his actions result in benefit to the community.

The objection to profit has its roots in the fallacy that one man's gain is another man's loss. This mistake is connected with the stupid theory that wealth is a limited thing, a fixed quantity, which must be equally divided among us. If it can be shown, and my case seems to me to show, that the making of a profit means more profit all round, that the creation of a piece of wealth is simply a step towards the creation of much more wealth, the error of the argument against profit becomes apparent.

My profits, so far as I can see (and I have analysed them pretty closely), have never done anything but make profits for everybody. It is of the very first importance to me that the other man should make a profit. If someone who has supplied me with something fails to make a satisfactory profit out of the transaction, he will not supply me with any more, and I shall be in difficulties. The notion that the business man is engaged in screwing the price down to the point at which the other man loses will not bear examination. The business man knows perfectly well that unless every transaction that he makes is satisfactory to both parties to it, his business will come to an end.

I sometimes think that herein lies one of the weaknesses of the Jew. The native business ability of the Jewish race has done immense service to civilisation, but the wisdom of the Jew so often stops short of the other man's profit, and that constitutes a difference which seems somehow to mark him off from the rest.

There are, of course, excessive profits. Occasions arise when the real profiteer can and does practise extortion upon his victims, but such cases are generally traceable to restrictive arrangements, many of them designed to remove the evil which they only accentuate. High profits in a free market confer a real benefit upon it and upon the community. They induce competition, they increase supplies and thus produce economy. Something may be said for the economic effects of excessive profits in a limited market such as those made by a trust or a trade union, for in these circumstances the consumer is driven to alternatives. This is clearly shown by the history of printing in the last ten years. It is permissible to argue that the short-sighted policy of both masters and men has hastened the time when letterpress printing will be supplanted by photographic printing. I have already produced second editions of books by photography, being unable to bear the heavy terms of the printer at present prices. The day it would seem is not far distant when photography will take the place of the old method entirely. *The Blackpool Times* is only an instance in support of this view.

The same kind of thing is happening with the bricklayers, whose excessive profits are forcing the consumers to use concrete. Another illustration may be found in the rapid rise in the price of laundry work, which has become so expensive as to drive womenfolk to silk underwear, which they can wash themselves, and men to soft collars, which they can wear for a week. Excessive profits are therefore not the unmixed evil that on the face of it they appear to be.

No discussion on profits would be complete without a note on the essential difference between profit on capital and profit on turnover. The company making 20 or 30 per cent. dividend upon its capital is not neces-

sarily making an undue profit upon its turnover. If a
company displays no energy, possesses no initiative,
and is content to turn its capital over once a year, and
finally announces a 5 per cent. profit, little or no comment is made upon its operations. If, however, it
understands its business, shows skill and resource,
uses up-to-date methods, and turns over the same
capital five times a year, thus making 25 per cent.,
criticism is loud and furious; though the latter process would appear to be more truly in the interests
not only of the company but of the community as a
whole.

Soon after Mr. Ramsay MacDonald became Prime
Minister there was a railway strike, and one of the first
pronouncements made by the Government took the
form of a warning to butchers and other traders that
if, as a result of the strike, there was any attempt to
profiteer in meat or other food products, the Government would take action. That pronouncement was
received with pleasure and applause by the people. It
was considered a reasonable and proper pronouncement for a Government to make, and it demonstrates,
as well as any recent instance, the depth of the ignorance of the public generally on this question of profit.
It is deplorable that an institution with a reputation
for wisdom like the British Government should be able
to issue to a people with a reputation for intelligence a
pronouncement such as this, and that the matter should
go almost unchallenged. Look at it from the point of
view of the unfortunate butcher. Suppose for the sake
of argument that he is doing a trade of five tons of
meat a week. A most cursory examination of the facts
will show that the profit of the butcher rests in the sale
of the last five cwts. of meat in the week. His organisation, his premises, his general expenses are all arranged
upon the basis of five tons a week, and his life as a

butcher depends upon the successful sale of the whole of that quantity. Then comes the railway strike, and his weekly supplies are reduced to, let us say, three tons. That is a hardship to the public, for it involves a limitation of the consumption of meat, but it is disaster to the butcher. He must lose money. He dare not raise the price of the three tons to the figure he would ordinarily secure for the five, and if he ventures to make any upward movement at all in order to mitigate somewhat the losses he is bound to suffer, " the Government will take action."

What possible action can the Government take? What results could such action have but to accentuate the difficulty? The provision by the Government of machinery for collecting and distributing the meat must be a more expensive method than the utilisation of the butcher's organisation, and any action of the kind can only result in a heavier loss than ever. And yet, so warped has the public intelligence become in these matters that, while accepting as normal the refusal of the railwayman to carry the meat except on his own terms, it heaps obloquy and abuse upon the butcher who dares to reduce the loss inflicted upon him by however small a margin.

Profit-sharing has been the subject of a good deal of discussion and experiment in recent years, and in this connection I must admit an indefensible inconsistency. I practise profit-sharing. I have a scheme in operation in my firm that has worked extremely well for several years past. I began upon the assumption that a 10 per cent. dividend is the minimum return upon capital that can be regarded as satisfactory in a speculative business like publishing. I agreed that, if the profits were sufficient to pay more than 10 per cent., the salaried staff should receive a percentage upon their salaries equal to any excess of 10 per cent. paid in the way of dividend. As for some years past the dividend has been at the rate of $17\frac{1}{2}$ per cent., those members of my staff in receipt of fixed wages or salaries have received a " bonus " upon their earnings at the rate of $7\frac{1}{2}$ per cent. In my case there is probably more justification for profit-sharing than in most, because it is a fact that, in an intricate business like publishing, most of the members of the administrative staff can exercise some influence upon profits and losses. But in general, I think, it is absolutely unsound to share profits with a wage-earner.

To begin with, any such arrangement appears to admit that there is some connection between wages and profits; that the one is paid at the expense of the other, or vice-versa. This was Ruskin's mistake. Any such idea is, in my judgment, completely false. Wages and profits are two different things arising from two different sets of causes and should not be confused one with the other. It is, for instance, absurd to suggest that a porter on the Southern Railway can have any influence on the profits of that undertaking. People who want to travel to Birmingham do not go to Brighton in preference because of the superior charm of the Brighton railway porter. Short of declining to do the duty assigned to him to the best of his ability, the railwayman can exercise no influence one way or the other on profits. The same is true of the compositor or ledger clerk.

Approaching the argument from the other end, the same conclusions are reached. Bad management can make a loss out of the most conscientious and efficient work. It is not suggested that the worker should share that loss, nor is bad management accepted as a reason for the reduction of wages. Nevertheless, I practise profit-sharing, and, while believing it to be, in theory, thoroughly bad, I confess it is, in practice, in the nature of a gesture or a concession to those psychological and ethical influences which, notwithstanding all the economic theory on earth, are part of the problem of industrial success.

There is a much better road than the profit-sharing road, and that also I am trying to follow. It is the road along which the worker becomes a capitalist and an employer. It is the road which has been traversed to an extraordinary length in the United States. Nothing short of a financial revolution has taken place in that country in the last few years. The Edison Commonwealth Corporation is only one of hundreds of huge concerns which have established within the last ten years big departments for the purpose of selling stock and bonds to the working classes. It was told me in both New York and Chicago, when I was there in 1921, that there were in the United States eleven million owners of industrial stock. I have been working gently along these lines and have exercised all my influence to induce the members of my staff to invest in the capital stock of my company, with the result that at the present moment some £36,000 worth of shares in Benn Brothers, Ltd., are held by persons who are actually working in the business. This is the ideal position. The wage-earner should be during working hours a wage-earner, performing a given task for a given price. Theoretically and scientifically, it must be possible to assess the exact value of manual effort and to pay that exact value. Side by side with this the worker should, by investing savings in the capital of the business in which he is working, or in any other business for that matter, become himself a capitalist, and thus combine within himself the dual function.

VII

MAKING £1,000 IN A WEEK: THE IMPORTANCE OF THE RISK FACTOR

ONLY once in my life have I indulged in a gamble, a real gamble in that the risks were heavy and the game was one of which I had no particular experience. All business is, of course, to some extent a gamble, but the word cannot be applied properly to risks taken in the ordinary way of trade by persons qualified to judge of them, and therefore able to measure them with a certain degree of exactitude. In this particular gamble I had no data to go upon; indeed none existed. I had some idea of the possible outlay; I also knew the amount of the possible returns; but I had no means of judging how far my estimates of outlay would prove right in the light of experience, nor was anyone able to say what was the margin of error in the estimate of receipts.

In July, 1909, the Fleet paid a visit to the Thames, thus offering an opportunity, very rare in those days, for the citizens of London to have a look at the Navy about which they sang so lustily, for which they paid so readily, and of which they knew and saw so little. Great popular interest was taken in this event, and great preparations were made to enable the people to take advantage of the occasion.

The Fleet was stationed off Southend and Shoeburyness, and some scores of excursions were arranged by train to the former place. Others were made by steamer from London Bridge. For 5s. it was possible to make the return journey by rail to Southend and the tram trip along the mile and a quarter of Southend Pier, and to enjoy a couple of hours on board a pleasure steamer cruising round the ships of war.

These circumstances seemed to me to offer an opportunity for enterprise in the way of making arrangements to meet the requirements of those who would be willing to spend a little more money, in order to avoid the crush and crowd of the more popular excursions which, until I entered the field, were the only means available for visiting the Fleet. I had, by a coincidence, spent an afternoon a few months earlier walking round the Isle of Grain and had inspected Port Victoria, a place with a good name but consisting only of a wooden pier and a railway siding. Port Victoria had not been in use since the London, Chatham and Dover and South-Eastern Railways had first experimented in the modern craze for amalgamation and the elimination of competition. The Continental service which once ran from Port Victoria had been discontinued, and the port and siding were almost derelict. But the name was good. Queen Victoria had on occasion used the port, and that was a point with a natural appeal to the advertising man.

I approached the South-Eastern and Chatham Railway and ascertained that it would be possible, though at a price which seemed to me exorbitant, to run special trains from Charing Cross to Port Victoria, and as a result of further negotiations I was able to issue the following prospectus:

Many thousands of Londoners and almost as many visitors from the country and abroad will be rushing to the river during the five days beginning July 19th, to take the very rare opportunity which then offers of inspecting the Fleet in the Thames. There will be assembled in the mouth of the river no fewer than 150 ships of war. The official programme shows that the great majority of the ships will be grouped between Southend and Port Victoria, where, counting the submarines, there are to be as many as five lines abreast. The total length of the main Fleet, from the destroyers off Leigh Middle to the eastern end of the Home and Atlantic Fleets off Shoeburyness Sands will be about twenty miles. The ships to be seen, including those in the upper reaches, will comprise 24 battleships, 16 armoured cruisers, 6 second-class cruisers, 7 special service ships, 7 scouts and third-class cruisers, 1 torpedo gunboat, 47 destroyers, 6 torpedo boats, and 35 submarines.

Never before in history has such a sight been so readily accessible, and it is unlikely that a similar event will occur during the lifetime of the present generation. Every description of river craft will be pressed into the service, and great difficulty will be experienced in obtaining accommodation by those who wish to avoid the crush and crowd and see the Fleet with some degree of comfort.

It is to meet the requirements of this class that the magnificent steamer, jointly owned by the L.B. & S.C. and L. & S.W. Railways, *Duchess of Fife*, has been specially chartered. The *Duchess of Fife* will be the best appointed passenger steamer in the river, and offers the only prospect of inspecting the Fleet in luxury and comfort.

Of the 150 ships to be seen, there will be between the Tower and Southend only 17, and these of the smaller descriptions. Visitors travelling by steamer from London will thus have to cover nearly 50 miles of the river and spend about three hours before they reach the main body of the Fleet, and there will also be this unattractive route to be traversed on the return journey.

The fast special trains of the Port Victoria Route make it possible, without starting early in the morning and returning late at night, to see all that is worth seeing and to avoid the uninteresting and tedious passage down and up the Thames.

Although the *Duchess of Fife* is licensed to carry a large number of persons, each day's party will be strictly limited, so as to ensure an entire absence of crush, perfect comfort, and an uninterrupted view of the line of ships.

Being built for the rough seas of the English Channel, the *Duchess of Fife* offers exceptional security from risk and from discomfort while cruising in the river and round the Fleet.

Lunch and light refreshment by Messrs. Spiers and Pond, Ltd., will be served each day, at moderate prices, in the magnificent saloon. Afternoon tea may be taken in the saloon or upon the promenade decks.

The number of passengers being strictly limited, as explained above, immediate application for tickets is essential. Tickets, if applied for before July 10, will cost £1 5s. each for Monday, Wednesday, Thursday, and Friday, or £1 11s. 6d. for Tuesday, on which day the Lord Mayor of London and the City Corporation make their official visit.

Out of this very rash gamble I secured much useful experience. It will be noticed that I priced my trip at 25s. and 31s. 6d., while the market figure for a similar service via Southend varied from 5s. to 10s. My forecast proved right, and I sold every ounce of accommodation I had, from which I learnt that cheapness is not always a necessary feature in a successful transaction. But the experience which has been of most value to me lay in the negotiating and the price I paid for the *Duchess of Fife*.

Brought up in a competitive market and thoroughly believing in the value of competition, when it came to chartering a steamer, I went to half a dozen brokers and agents in the shipping business and told them all my requirements. In my simplicity it seemed to me that they would each be anxious to secure the order and would produce, one after the other, steamers for my inspection, each cheaper than the last. But I overlooked the fact that there is not an unlimited supply of pleasure steamers available for such a purpose as I had in view; that most of those existing were already engaged on the Southend side of the river; and that, in view of the superior quality of the excursion I proposed to advertise, it was necessary to have a steamer with an attractive reputation and adequate accommodation. As I learnt afterwards, there was in fact only one such vessel to be had nearer than the Clyde, and the voyage from that river was, for my brief purpose, out of the question.

As has been mentioned, the ship I finally secured belonged jointly to the London, Brighton and South Coast and London and South-Western Railways, and was used for trips between Portsmouth and the Isle of Wight. My numerous shipping agents all fastened upon her; all made bids for her; and were all informed that she was much in demand, that there were many inquiries, and that she could only be obtained if the contract were signed at once. The price for a week's hire would be £850, plus the victualling of the crew, coal, and insurance. I had, in fact, made a market against myself, and subsequently formed the opinion that I could have had the craft with victuals and coal and insurance for £500 had I but grasped more completely the subtle workings of the thing called " competition." I did not till then realise that there may be competition to buy as well as competition to sell. This experience with the *Duchess of Fife* has helped me since on many occasions to an understanding of the reason why, whenever a public body requires to make a purchase, it always has to pay very much more than the real value for what it wants.

It remains to explain how I, a young publisher with every penny that I possessed sunk in my own business, and carrying, in addition, an incubus of debt, was able to undertake a gamble involving formidable risks and sums of money which were, for me, distinctly large. The best estimate that I could make out of the outlay necessary to finance the trip was somewhere between £5,000 and £6,000. That was the total outlay. Should the scheme prove a complete failure, £4,000 or £5,000 might be lost. Should it, on the other hand, prove successful in every way, I conjectured a possible profit of £2,000.

In view of my financial position and responsibilities, I sought out a relative who was more fortunately placed and, having succeeded in persuading him that the scheme was a good one, we went into partnership on the matter. The terms of arrangement between us were very simple: I was to do all the work, he was to find all the money—and we were to share the profits. He took all responsibility in the event of loss. The business was conceived and carried to a finish in a period of less than three weeks. The actual work associated with it was done mostly within the space of seven days. I have never before or since done such a week's work. I had my clothes off twice in seven nights. The staff of the syndicate consisted of two clerks borrowed from my business. A room was hired and two telephones installed (it being possible in those days to get a telephone at a few hours' notice). Quantities of tickets and bills of advertisement had to be printed, and all this part of the business, from the writing out and ordering to the printing and even delivery, was executed within the space of twenty-four hours. The printing trade had not at that time been organised into its present state of leisurely efficiency.

There is no need at this distance of time to tell the story in all its details, but it will readily be believed that a good deal of trouble and anxiety was associated with it. The South-Eastern Railway even in those days had its little weaknesses. I well remember how one of our evening trips, which should have returned my 600 passengers to Charing Cross at the convenient hour of 11 p.m. landed them at Cannon Street at 4 a.m., with the result that I was inundated with claims for hotel accommodation, cabs to the most distant parts of the suburbs, and other forms of damage. But we surmounted these little difficulties and came out of the gamble at the end of the week with a very handsome profit; my partner and I taking a trifle less than £1,000 each.

My purpose in telling the story is, of course, to consider and discuss its economic implications, to discover to what extent I was justified in making this large sum of money, and whether good or harm resulted from this profitable speculation, so definitely stigmatised by Ruskin as " sin." From that point of view my partner would perhaps be considered a greater sinner than I, for he did no work. He received £1,000 simply by virtue of the fact that he owned a little money and was therefore able to shoulder the risk of the enterprise. His case is rendered blacker still from the interesting circumstance that, from beginning to end of the whole business, he did not part with a penny-piece. The terms of his arrangement with me provided that he should find any money that was wanted, but, as things turned out, the money from the sale of tickets began to come in before we were called upon to pay any of our liabilities. The syndicate therefore carried through its affairs without in fact possessing a single cent of capital. I could, of course, have carried through the business without a partner at all. I could have pawned my estate, and no doubt someone would have been willing to lend me £4,000 or £5,000 on more or less reasonable terms, had I been plucky enough to risk all my possessions on this little enterprise. I am, however, made of more cautious stuff, and that method did not seem wise. I therefore sought the assistance of my partner, and, as will be seen, the enterprise depended entirely upon him. Without the existence of someone who was in a position and willing to risk the loss of £5,000, the *Duchess of Fife* trips would never have been available to the public. My partner shouldered that risk.

From my point of view the most important result was that it removed a purchasing power of one thousand sovereigns from the pockets of some thousands of people into my own. That would not seem to be of great significance from the point of view of public benefit. In this case, however, some importance did attach to it. The existence of £1,000 worth of purchasing power in the pockets of a large number of fairly well-to-do people was, of course, a useful thing for industry generally. It meant that goods to the value of £1,000, coming from many markets, could be purchased and, in every case, that expenditure would involve so much employment and so much profit. But the transference of all those little fragments of purchasing power to me in one big lump of £1,000 did, as a matter of fact, alter the character of that sum, by taking it out of the current account of the spending public and placing it to the credit of my capital account, where it promptly became part of the capital with the help of which I have been able to develop and enlarge my business.

It can, I think, be safely argued that this £1,000, considered as part of the general well-being of the community, is doing better service in promoting business enterprise than if it had been spent in single sovereigns by a thousand people who would have bought a number of isolated commodities.

Even so, this gamble of mine went further and deeper than that. It added, in the course of the week over which it was spread, some £4,000 to the wages fund, and it had the special effect of stiffening the market in the wages of seamen, coal-workers, railwaymen, and engineers. It is obvious and incontrovertible that but for the presence of that £4,000 on the market, competing for the services of all these workers, the market must have been weaker and the wages of all of them less. We can go further back and justify the transaction by considering the case of the business men and the speculators who, years before, had put up their savings and risked them upon the building of the steamer which I used. Those wages, for the construction of the ship, the making of the steel and all the other processes involved in it, would never have been paid had it not been for the expectation that people like myself would be willing later on to speculate still further in the use of the vessel. So, whether the transaction is considered backwards or forwards, it will be seen to be a great wage-producing agent, causing in its history much more activity and the use of far greater sums of money in a bigger scheme of things than ever appeared on my little account.

This venture with the *Duchess of Fife* is the only big gamble completely outside my own line of business in which I have ever indulged, but I have lost a great deal more money than I made in this way on other small speculations indirectly associated with publishing. Chief among these were two exhibitions that at different times I was tempted to conduct. An old and respected friend of mine, Mr. John T. Day, proprietor of *The Shoe and Leather Record*, had for many years past organised a very successful trade exhibition, the Shoe and Leather Fair. He had shown that it is possible to associate a trade paper with a trade exhibition, and that the two things, conducted together, can benefit the trade, the public, and the publisher. If John T. Day could do this, it seemed to me that I might be equally successful. So in 1898, when I was running *The House*, a journal concerned with the decoration of the home, I attempted to organise an exhibition of domestic art at the Imperial Institute. I was fortunate in securing the patronage of King Edward, then Prince of Wales, and I surrounded the enterprise with all the glamour of a distinguished committee, which included many leaders of the society of that day. But I was wrong. Whether it was that the Imperial Institute did not conjure up in the minds of the public the idea of success, or whether it was that the public in those days did not care enough about domestic art, the fact remains that the applications for space from prospective exhibitors were not sufficient to enable us to open the doors. The exhibition was never held, and a few hundred pounds were lost.

In 1911 I tried again, entering into a contract to hire Olympia and run a hardware exhibition. As the proprietor of one of the most successful hardware papers in the world, I thought, judging again by the experience of John T. Day, that it would be a simple thing for me to do. Something, however, though to this day I do not understand what it was, made it appear to the hardware trade that I was not the person to do this work, and my previous experience was repeated. The prospectus failed to enlist enough support, and the preliminary expenses had to be written off.

All this only shows that the work of supplying public needs, or of making the public recognise its needs, is not so simple as would-be organisers of society appear to imagine.

The Socialist theories overlook entirely the intricate question of risk. They conveniently ignore the fact that before anything can be done to produce a single article for public use, some person or some agency must undertake the risk of loss necessarily involved. No system can ever ensure that, when the article is made, the public will be willing to accept it at the value put upon it by those who make it. Hence, in any system allowing any choice at all to the buyer or consumer, there must always be the risk that in the end loss will be incurred. Risk is the very heart and core of commerce, and yet it is this factor to which least attention is paid by those who are so fond of discussing the rights and wrongs of the industrial system.

There is, of necessity, a certain amount of risk connected with business of every kind. When the village grocer buys a hundredweight of sugar, hoping to retail

I

it in pounds and half-pounds to the villagers, he takes many little risks. The sugar may not sell, or it may take a long time to sell. His assistant may drop water in it or spill it on the floor of the warehouse and waste it; it may be stolen, mice may eat it, and a hundred other things may happen to cause him loss. He, therefore, consciously or unconsciously, adds to the retail price of the sugar some small fraction to cover his risk. His neighbour, the village draper, takes a rather heavier risk in dealing with millinery. He has to face the possibility of changing fashions, the vicissitudes of the weather, and so forth, and these together make it necessary for him to charge rather more in respect of his risk than the grocer. The merchant who sells timber to a builder for delivery six months hence, thus enabling the builder to enter into a contract for the erection of a warehouse, takes a longer and larger risk which must be proportionately covered. The publisher of a book usually charges twice as much as he otherwise need, if he were certain that he could sell out his whole edition, and yet it is not alleged that publishers as a class make too much money; the fact being that the double price is not more than sufficient to cover the cost of the books which nobody buys.

My financial backer in the very profitable deal which I have described did not, therefore, get more than a justifiable profit considering the heavy nature of his risk. All the profits on all such deals, balanced with all the losses, would disclose a surprisingly small surplus, and when it is remembered that in a long business career this single transaction produced the only profit of the kind that I can put on record, it will be seen how really big was the risk of loss involved.

I have tried to show that wealth is exchange, and the story of the *Duchess of Fife* may help some to understand that the most difficult work in connection with exchange, and therefore wealth production, is the shouldering of the risk inseparable from every commercial undertaking.

It is a misunderstanding of this vital question of risk-taking which leads to much wrong thinking on speculation and gambling. It is probably true that England's greatness, that our lead in the creation of the commerce of the world, is due to the fact that we possess in a rather more pronounced degree than most people the speculative or the gambling instinct. My partner in the *Duchess of Fife* venture was a speculator. He had a few thousand pounds, no doubt invested in gilt-edged securities producing to him, in those days, 2½ or 3 per cent., and he was willing to risk the loss of his capital on the chance that he might increase it and secure a larger income. He wanted his gamble and did very well out of it in this particular case, but, were he given to speculation of this kind as a habit, there is little doubt that he would lose in the long run.

The onus of risk is regarded altogether too lightly and assessed far too cheaply, notwithstanding the profits made by some who take such risks as I have described. "The overweening conceit," says Adam Smith, "which the greater part of men have of their own abilities is an ancient evil remarked by the philosophers and moralists of all ages. Their absurd presumption in their own good fortune has been less taken notice of. It is, however, if possible, still more universal. There is no man living who, when in tolerable health and spirits, has not some share of it. The chance of gain is by every man more or less overvalued, and the chance of loss is by most men undervalued, and by scarce any man, who is in tolerable health and spirits, valued at more than it is worth." (*The Wealth of Nations.*)

I am not an expert on betting, but I am told that more money is lost at 20 or 30 to 1 than when, in the language of the turf, " odds are even." There is something in our mental outfit which finds a disproportionate attraction in a 30 to 1 chance and makes us willing to pay for it more readily than when the odds are 2 to 1, thus showing, as Adam Smith says, that the chance of loss is constantly underrated.

This question of speculation requires further examination. It is not realised as widely as it should be how much each one of us depends for his comfort, convenience, and security upon the speculator, who, of course, makes and maintains every market that there is. The business of the speculator is to ease the price of a commodity up or down, as required, thus relieving the rest of us of the grave risks and serious inconveniences to which we should be subjected if we ourselves had to shoulder the violent fluctuations of the market.

The dangers and liabilities incurred by those who assume responsibility for risks may, perhaps, be seen most clearly in connection with insurance.

Consider the case of a ship leaving London with a cargo for Australia. The professional speculator (who, as will be seen later, is not speculating in the sense in which the word is used by the public, but is really supplying the most essential ingredient in wealth production, the assumption of risk) knows from past experience that out of a thousand ships sailing from London for Australia, a definite percentage has come to grief. He is, therefore, able to offer a price for insuring the ship and its cargo—let us say 5s. per cent.

The insurance market, acting through one of its members, accepts 5s., and for that sum undertakes to pay £100 if the ship should be lost on its way. Half-way through the voyage it is reported from some passing vessel that the ship in question is experiencing engine trouble. The insurance market knows from experience that ships suffering in this way fail to reach their destination in a much heavier proportion than others. The odds, therefore, alter and the price to insure such a ship becomes heavier, let us say 25s. per cent. The speculator on the insurance market who has accepted 5s. promptly reinsures the vessel with some other speculator at 25s. and loses £1 per cent.

Presently, reports come through that the engine trouble is more serious than at first appeared. The chances of a successful voyage being more remote, the proper rate for insurance, judged by the best experience, becomes £5 per cent. Thereupon the speculator who has taken the 25s. rate reinsures with another speculator at £5 and loses £3 15s. Day by day the news grows worse, and day by day the rate goes up until, the ship being a month overdue and no news of her having reached the market for weeks, hope of her safe arrival becomes very slender, the chances are indeed 19 to 1 against her surviving at all, and some speculator accepts £95 for the risk of paying £100 if she should prove a total loss.

In the end, one of two things happens: either the ship is never heard of, or she puts in a belated appearance in an Australian port. In the first event, the total cost of the ship and cargo has been spread over a large number of professional speculators, without the existence of whom the ship would never have sailed; its cargo could never have been sold to Australia, and the whole enterprise must have failed to materialise unless, indeed, it is argued that we should go back to the days of Antonio, when one man was willing to risk the whole of a large fortune on a big enterprise, and when big business transactions were few and far between. In the second event, that of the ship arriving safely but late, the fortunate speculator who received the £95 to take the risk of £100 pockets his good, fat premium.

Even then, however, he has made in the normal way no more profit than is necessary for the conduct of his business. He is, on the insurance market, a professional taker of heavy risks, of last hopes, and the experience of the market is sufficient to show that this speculator, taking day by day 19 to 1 chances, makes no more than a normal profit.

A moment's consideration will show that, without the speculator, no forward contract is possible. Many of our current troubles are due to the excessive risk engendered by post-War conditions and the lack of a sufficient number of speculators to bear the burden of these risks.

As an example, before the War it was my practice to buy my printing paper on three-year contracts. It was usual for the paper-maker to quote a price for deliveries which he would undertake to maintain for a period of three years. The paper-maker, working in those days on very narrow margins, could not himself assume responsibility for any extreme fluctuations in the prices of materials which might occur during a period of three years. He relied upon the professional speculator on the markets from which he drew his supplies. To quote a price for paper three years ahead involved, among many other conditions, an assurance of pulp and freights from Canada or Norway at firm prices during the whole of that period. Two tons of coal go to the making of every ton of paper, and my maker, in giving me his price, had to be sure that for three full years he could rely upon receiving his coal at a fixed figure, notwithstanding strikes or other contingencies. The same conditions applied to the supply of china clay and all his other requirements. The three-year contract was a great convenience to me as a publisher. Assured of my paper supply at a fixed price for a reasonable period, I could make my plans and develop my business in a way that is not possible to-day, when, thanks to political uncertainty and other legacies of the War, we have to be content to think at the most a few months ahead.

In those days, therefore, I relied for the stability of my business upon many professional speculators, who had undertaken all the several risks associated with a fixed price for my paper.

The whole question is, of course, exceedingly complex and demands a far more rigid and meticulous examination than would be appropriate here; but it would be wrong to leave the reader with the impression that the professional speculator who undertook the delivery of coal three years ahead at a fixed price was in any real sense gambling. As a member of his market, fulfilling his proper function, it would be his duty, when signing that contract, to find on the other side a coalowner who wished to be sure of a market for his output in three years' time, and who could, on that guarantee, see his way to employ sufficient labour to develop his pits.

The same considerations apply to the erection of a building such as I am now putting up in Fleet Street. As I write, my position is that I shall want large supplies of steel in three months' time, quantities of bricks in six months, and deliveries of timber in twelve. But I could not put up my building unless some contractor were able to assure me that he would do the work and place the new offices at my disposal at a given date for a given price. I should certainly never be justified in embarking upon an extensive building scheme if threatened with the risk that, when the steelwork was put up, I might discover that the price of bricks had doubled and that I had not the money with which to buy them. I am absolutely dependent upon the professional speculator, who, standing in the middle of the market, accepts my difficulties, balances them against the similar difficulties of the suppliers of materials, and thus makes the operations of both sides possible.

There is a common misapprehension here which requires correcting. It is assumed that risk-taking and gambling are one and the same thing. Nothing could be farther from the truth. The line between the two is very easily drawn. The risk-taker, the most valuable of all the functionaries who help to develop wealth-producing industries, renders a service to others, in return for which he hopes to receive a profit. The gambler renders no such service. Any doubt, therefore, as to whether a particular transaction is legitimate or not can be settled at once by applying the test of service.

Risk-taking and speculation illustrate, perhaps better than any other examples, the real trouble with Capitalism and capitalistic systems, namely, the stupidity of the business classes as a whole. They have allowed the impression to become widespread and general that there is a large class of persons making big fortunes at the expense of the community by gambling in the commodities upon which the rest of us depend. Nothing could be more inaccurate. That there are such gamblers and that they occasionally make money cannot be denied. These, however, constitute a very small class, and, further, it is beyond doubt that, on the whole, they lose more than they make. Monte Carlo is kept going and made rich because, as the song tells us, there was once a " man who broke the bank," but it cannot be argued from this isolated fact that the people who frequent the tables at that fascinating holiday resort make money.

The professional speculator in stocks and shares is the first person who jumps to the average mind when mention is made of the much-misunderstood subject of speculation. It is commonly assumed that, if a man can gain admission to the Stock Exchange, he is then able with little effort to make big money by a process which the public, in its carelessness and ignorance, is content to dismiss as a species of gambling. Nobody bothers to inquire what would happen if one of us, having saved £25 and wanting to invest it in London County Council 3 per cents., were to canvass the streets and houses of the metropolis to discover a person who happened to conform to the three parts of our particular necessity, namely, that, in the first place, he should possess L.C.C. 3 per cents.; secondly, that he should be in a position to sell them; and, thirdly, that, owning exactly £25 worth of them, he should be willing to sell. Nor does anyone trouble to inquire how, if we went through this laborious process, the price of the L.C.C. 3 per cents. would be settled; while all the machinery of transfer and exchange would seem to be beneath the consideration of the critics of this Stock Exchange transaction. The much-maligned speculator, who makes a hard-earned living out of L.C.C. 3 per cents., has a long and weary road to travel and a complicated business to learn before he can carry on his nefarious practices at all.

Just like any other shopkeeper, he must first of all make it known that he is there. Further, it must be known that he proposes to specialise in municipal stocks and shares, so that those who want industrials or foreign bonds will not go to him, any more than people who want meat go to a chemist. When he has thus established himself as a recognised dealer in municipal issues, he must stand in the market and be prepared to buy or sell everything that comes along. From an intimate knowledge of the exact position of the various issues he must judge how much is likely to come to the market; how many buyers and how many sellers there will be; and what is the price at which business can be done to the satisfaction of both parties. Accordingly he will announce a figure which seems to him to be appropriate for L.C.C. 3 per cents. If that figure is an attractive one from the point of view of the holders of this particular stock, they will tend to rush upon the market to sell to him, but the buyers whom he must find to balance his account will hold back, and he will be threatened with the risk of accepting large quantities of the stock at a price which other people will not pay. Finding himself in that position he lowers the price, marks the stock down, and in this way checks sellers and encourages buyers. Day by day and hour by hour this delicate process is performed, always discovering that happy mean which exactly suits the points of view of both buyers and sellers, and makes it possible for both to deal freely in the stock in question. The London County Council is consequently able to borrow money which it could never obtain without the professional speculator who gives to each investor a guarantee that his investment is always liquid and realisable. The public does not invest in gilt-edged securities and accept a low rate of interest without the certain assurance that it can always realise its investment rapidly. That is an essential condition in cheap public borrowing.

The best illustration I can give of the common errors of thought on this matter of business speculation and its general benefits to the community is a speech I heard some years ago from the lips of Mr. Ben Tillett. He was younger, less experienced and a little wilder than he has since become. He was discussing the wrongs of Capitalism and the way in which the rich lived in luxury by grinding the faces of the poor. He waxed very eloquent about the wealth that was made at the expense of the workers' stomachs and took by way of illustration the people's bread. According to him, this common necessity was permitted to the poor folk, whom he represented, only after the money-owners, the gamblers, and the speculators had squeezed great fortunes out of it. He traced the history of the loaf from the time that the land which grows the wheat was bought and sold in Canada. First wealth was amassed from speculations in land. Then the seed to be sown was subject to speculation in the Pit at Chicago. Millionaires were sprung from the very seed that the starving poor in the East End of London needed to provide them with bread. The crops were at last grown and further fortunes arose out of the buying and selling of them. Shipping magnates gambled in freights as part of the operation of bringing the grain from the wheat-fields of Canada to the London market. Millers, again, bought and sold it, at every turn adding to its price. Throughout the whole proceeding there was the middleman carrying on the scoundrelly business of buying and selling and robbing the worker of the bread which God has provided for his sustenance.

The reader who remembers Ben Tillett at his best will be able to reconstruct the wonderful picture which that great orator could draw from such a story.

The occasion was one of those conferences between capital and labour with which I have been closely associated, and it was my painful duty to follow Tillett and to spoil the work of art which he had so skilfully wrought. A few sentences were sufficient for the purpose. It so happened that, at the time when Tillett was working up the indignation of the ignorant on speculation in grain and bread, there was a statesman of almost equal eloquence, Joseph Chamberlain, leading a great party whose principal grievance was that the loaf was too big, that the Empire was going to pieces because of the low price of bread. We were assured that in order to win salvation our food must cost us more.

I do not remember any single case that demonstrates more clearly and conclusively the real purpose and effect of speculation. Speculation, like competition, is a price-reducer, a big force for economy, and one of the greatest services that the development of the economic system has rendered to mankind.

So it can be seen that those who object to what is called the incentive of gain, to the acquisitive instinct ordinarily supposed to be at the back of industrial enterprise, those who think that society could be so conducted that profit making could be eliminated, have yet to explain how they will rid us of the risks and the losses. If all the books and articles that have been written about the iniquity of private gain were re-written round the subject of private loss, the writers of most of them would, of necessity, be driven to different conclusions. This personal desire, individual greed, so much discussed and so much dissected, is in fact an immense power, working through millions of private individuals, for the preservation of society from losses which, if allowed free play, would soon bring it to an end. When losses and profits are balanced; when it is shown that, notwithstanding all the profits, these are mostly absorbed in the losses; when it is shown that the owners of the profits, whatever their desires, take no more than a very small margin which is barely sufficient to provide us with the increase of savings and capital upon which our progress depends, then it seems to me that the case against private enterprise and individual gain entirely disappears.

VIII

COMPANY PROMOTING AND OTHER BUSINESS SECRETS

THE life of a business man does not lend itself to graphic description. Buying and selling does not make good " copy." A man who stands behind the counter and serves out cabbages need not look for notoriety. If his cabbages are good, if his manners give no offence, if he refrains from excessive drink and conducts himself with ordinary propriety, he will in time be known as a " respected resident "; but in the main his life will pass without comment, and his only obituary notice will be the inscription on his gravestone. The man who wants to be somebody, on the other hand, and to produce good biographical material, must eat other people's cabbages and devote himself to agitation. He must make speeches, and write to the papers. He must rail in public about the tenure of the land which produces the cabbages, expatiate on the mode of life of the man who sells the cabbages, or the man who brings them to market: he can, if he will, stir to its depths the public indignation over the price at which the cabbages are sold. In each, or any, of these ways he can become an infinitely more important person than the humdrum individual who merely sees that his fellows are provided with appropriate cabbages. The result of his work as an agitator may be to halve the supply of cabbages, to drive the cabbage merchant out of business; to produce conditions in which only the professional profiteer can venture to touch cabbages; to create artificial restrictions and regulations—in short, to ruin the industry. All this will make for greatness. The more public inconvenience caused by descanting on these questions, the higher will be the public estimate of the professional agitator. It would seem to be essential to make trouble, or at least to be associated with trouble, if you would become a great public character and leave behind a great biography. There is no good copy in the day by day or year by year monotony of an ordinary business career.

I have several times lately kept a note of the details of one day's work, and I have been driven to the conclusion at the end of each day that I have done nothing but say " Yes " and " No " to a large number of people, and, in their view, been accordingly a help or a nuisance. As will have been noticed from earlier pages, I have at various times done some of the practical work of every department of the publishing business. But it is undoubtedly true of my present position that I do little that would be recognised in most of the political schemes of industrial and social reconstruction. I merely say " Yes " and " No." An eight-year-old child of mine paid a visit to my office some little time ago, and went home and explained to the family what a farce business really is. " Daddy rang a bell," he told them, " a man came in with a piece of paper on which Daddy scribbled his name, ever so badly, and then he put his hat on and said he might not be back to-day." My function is to take the risk, a function discussed in some detail in the previous chapter. In the course of fulfilling this function I lose and make a certain amount of money every week of my life. In the end the profits are, or have so far proved, greater than the losses, and for this reason I am considered successful. But my chief work to-day consists in saying " Yes " and " No," and thereby taking the risk of loss or profit arising from the actions of the various people whom I control.

The whole burden of my story is that these essential activities are, and always would be, totally impossible without the existence of some such person as myself, exercising an office which, from its very nature, cannot be separated from the private or individual gain to which my opponents in economic thought take such grave exception.

An essential to success in a business career would seem to be the ability to say " No," and the knowledge of when to say it. Although in the minds of those who know my business I am associated with considerable activity, it is all merely a result of the very occasional " Yes " compared with the much more usual " No." If the business man were to say " Yes " to more than a very small percentage of the proposals made to him, he would not remain in business long.

" No " is the most important word in the language and is the most difficult word of all to say. The education of the child consists very largely in " No," but it is not easy to say it in most cases. The business man must always be saying " No " to the worker, " No " to the supplier, and " No " to the customer—the last operation being perhaps the most difficult and the least understood of the three.

It is very difficult to decline a request for a 5 per cent. discount on a prospective customer's account, especially when one is told that all one's competitors give it and that without it the account will not be opened. Given the chance of an order of the value of £100 at one's advertised price, subjected only to 5 per cent. discount, it needs a strong and good business man to throw away £95 for the sake of the principle involved in a five-pound note. Yet if business is to be sound and honest that must be done. It is essential to be fair and just to one's customers. If your price for a given article is £100 and you sell to one customer at that price and then, because the next is gifted with superior bargaining power, you allow him to have the same article for £95, you are surely wronging the first man.

I have 20,000 customers on my advertising ledgers. When I first entered the trade paper business, a fixed price was the exception rather than the rule. The price of each advertisement was the subject of negotiation. That is, even to-day, very largely the case with many small papers, and it is one of the reasons why they remain small. Apart, however, from the justice of the matter, it would be a physical impossibility to arrange individual terms with 20,000 customers. So it becomes evident that, even in a matter like this, honesty is still the best policy; and, by developing the courage to say " No," and declining to do business except upon very definite and rigid terms, one is not only able to deal honestly and fairly with all one's customers, but to expand one's business.

A good deal might be said about the science of saying " No." In the business of buying and selling, even in its simplest forms, the buyer must say " No " on the first offer of the seller, if only as a means of testing the quality of the article or proposition, and hearing more about it. But the most difficult " No " of all is that which must be said to some enthusiastic assistant who, out of his desire to help and his personal ambition, has evolved some new idea which will not work. It is very necessary in these cases to say the " No " in such a way as not to discourage more ideas of the right kind, and the difficulty is not made any less by the suspicion that will always lurk, certainly in the mind of your assistant and possibly in your own, that after all your decision may be wrong.

For the head of a business, as for the head of a family, it is very necessary to be sure when saying " Yes " or " No " that he is not being used as a court of appeal from some lesser authority. When your child comes to you with a request to be allowed to sit up to supper, if you are a wise and practised father, you do not answer the question until you have ascertained whether an answer has already been secured from Mother. Similarly, in the running of a business, a minor official may come to you with a question or suggestion, having no other purpose in view than to take your decision back in triumph to his superior, who has already passed judgment in the opposite sense.

I suppose there is no more dreadful secret associated with the conduct of business than what is called the " Capital Account." It is generally to be found written in the private ledger, which is provided with an elaborate lock and key and guarded behind the heavy doors of the private office safe. It is in capital arrangement and manipulation that the making of fortunes largely consists, and I have done my share in this connection. So that, in discussing business secrets, it is right and proper that I should have something to say about that process of secret scheming in shares and stocks and goodwills which to most people is a closed book, and to many suggests practices which, to put it mildly, are regarded as doubtful. The capital account of a newspaper is the flimsiest thing there is. As a general rule a newspaper requires a backing of good, solid capital, but when this is invested and the property is established, all this capital assumes the nebulous form of goodwill and consists of nothing at all except profit-earning capacity. There are newspapers (and some of mine are among them) which never had much solid capital at their back, which have grown by slow stages over long periods and, having acquired

K

large earning capacities, have thereby also acquired large capital values. But whether values have their origin in actual money put in and sunk, or whether no money was there in the beginning, does not matter at all in considering the capital value of a newspaper enterprise at any particular time; for value rests entirely upon the profit-making capacity of the publication. I am speaking, of course, of publications and newspapers as commercial propositions. The value of any of my properties is at any time merely the index of its capacity for earning an annual income. A newspaper, therefore, demonstrates clearly the illusory nature of capital.

The best illustration that I can give of the many operations on capital account which have passed through my hands is the way in which I handled the purchase and sale of the Electrician Printing and Publishing Co. This was a business established in 1864 by Sir John Pender, Sir James Anderson, and others interested in the new science of electrical telegraphy, with the object of publishing a newspaper known as *The Electrician* for the development and expansion of that science. The business seems to have flourished and to have accomplished the work designed for it. As electricity became more and more generally applied, the paper became a leading authority on electrical matters. The Pender interests gradually disappeared, and in 1898 the journal became the sole property of a Mr. George Tucker, who, I am informed, had joined it years previously as an apprentice and had gradually risen to the top. Mr. Tucker was a Victorian type of business man and he added very largely to the original idea of an electrical newspaper. He developed by degrees a large printing establishment, added other journals and piled up department upon department, doing the business of an advertising agent and a wholesale stationer as well as any work coming his way as a general jobbing printer.

When I came into touch with the company, it was employing about 250 people. At the lower prices of those days, it had a turnover of about £25,000 a year and was making almost no profit. I had for years coveted *The Electrician*. It fitted in with the guiding principle of my career, the massing together of trade papers, and so I kept in touch with Mr. Tucker and discussed with him from time to time the possibility of his selling me the copyright.

Nothing happened, however. Mr. Tucker was much older than I, and his ideas differed widely from mine. It may be accepted as a general rule that the older the man the longer he takes to come to a decision. On the whole it may be that the older man is wiser than the very young one who takes perhaps a premature decision, but in this case it meant that by the time I did secure the business it had sunk to its lowest ebb.

I had no desire for the printing works and the sundry other activities of Mr. Tucker, and my negotiations with him were confined to the question of purchasing *The Electrician*. In 1914 Mr. Tucker died and left his affairs in the hands of the Public Trustee, and it was then that I was thrown into one of those company-promoting capital-manipulation operations which are so little understood and so much suspected by critics of the economic organisation of things.

The Public Trustee would consider nothing short of the sale in one lot of the whole of the Tucker interest. I had, therefore, to purchase a tangled miscellany of enterprises and unravel from it the particular one which I desired. The Public Trustee's price was £12,000. The price which had been discussed between Mr. Tucker and myself for the newspaper alone was £5,000. I could manage the latter figure but not the former. After much negotiation I bought the business for £12,000, £5,000 of which I found on my own account by borrowing from the bank, and £7,000 was put up by my friends.

Then began a long process of reorganisation and reconstruction, and my financial reward was considerable, and, in accordance with the dictates of Pareto's Law, everyone associated with the enterprise, from the top to the bottom, also benefited considerably. Mr. Tucker's management of the business had for the previous six years produced dividends on a very small capital of $3\frac{1}{2}$, $1\frac{1}{4}$, 3, $2\frac{1}{2}$, $3\frac{1}{2}$, and 2 per cent. The annual profits of the two enterprises, into which I split this concern, are now equivalent to the whole of the capital of the Tucker company. His small profits accompanied the lowest wages and the worst conditions that I have met with in my experience. My larger profits are associated with wages and conditions which, I take pride in thinking, are a little in advance of the comparatively high standard of these days.

My first act was to apply to the Electrician Printing and Publishing Co., Ltd., my principle that printing and publishing are two separate trades and should not be run together. I took over at once that part of the enterprise which could be classified as copyrights, with all the editorial and advertising members of the staff, and ran the weekly publications and the technical books as part of my own business. The effect was immediate and astonishing. *The Electrician*, surrounded with the machinery of a printing works, enjoyed a revenue from sales and advertisements of under £10,000 a year. In three or four years that figure reached over £25,000.

I then turned my attention to the printing establishment, sundry merchanting and agency business, a cumbersome affair in which I was not in the least interested. I had the good fortune to find associated with the concern a couple of men in managerial positions, one of whom had grown up with the business, and both of whom were working for small salaries under bad conditions out of personal regard for the old " governor," to whom, through long years of association, they had naturally become closely attached. These considerations did not enter into the relationship between them and me, and the death of Mr. Tucker, and my arrival on the scene as chief proprietor, gave opportunity for the development of ambitions and abilities which both men possessed and for which there had hitherto been no scope. I came to terms with them for the sale of that part of the business which I did not want. It was formed into a separate company; I capitalised it at a figure which left me a reasonable profit and, taking advantage of my experience of 1900, when, it will be remembered, I acquired a property on easy terms by means of long-dated bills, I sold this company to its two managers on a similar scheme. I am very happy to know that since those days this business has flourished apace. It has acquired other works and is now of a size and importance far exceeding anything that could have been foreseen in the days when I handled it. This only confirms my views as to the wisdom of specialisation.

The net result of all this manipulation is that in a short period of seven or eight years an old-fashioned business on the verge of bankruptcy, with a turnover of £25,000, employing 250 people on low wages, has been transformed into two flourishing separate concerns that turn over between them many times the figure of eight years ago and make, I believe, at both ends, handsome profits, to say nothing of an addition to the wages fund which cannot be less than £100,000 a year.

So far as I am concerned—and this is a piece of iniquity on which the " new world " mongers would focus their attention to the exclusion of anything else

—I came out of the deal with an addition to my capital of £3,000 or £4,000, which, however, is not really capital at all, but a figure which fixes my share of the profits of the enterprise as a whole, or my commission for having been the agent of this beneficial transaction.

But I am searching for business secrets. It is commonly supposed that business is one maze of secrets; a supposition that is now largely false. There is no more absurd hoax than the business " secret," and the idea should be knocked out of the public mind. It consists to a large extent in the gifts or innate qualities of individuals. Thus, a very important secret of success in business rests in understanding the art of employing, in the power to attract to oneself others who are willing to carry out their duties as directed with efficiency and goodwill, the one being almost as important as the other.

The objection to the employer, voiced so loudly by the Socialist and felt to some extent by everybody, has its roots in the fact that he has it in his power to bring employment to an end, to discharge, to " sack." The secret of employing successfully lies in a proper appreciation of this right. All too few employers take their privilege seriously enough. Many of them indeed fail woefully to grasp the fact that they are employers at all. A man will set up as a manufacturer of furniture and his mind, absorbed in the technicalities of his trade, becomes oblivious of the fact that he is not only a manufacturer but also an employer. His function is not only to manufacture furniture but to employ people. If he is so presumptuous as to think that he is able to find employment for others, he should continually bear that fact in mind and not allow it to be entirely subservient to his more obvious purpose, the manufacture of furniture. He should regard his duty as an employer so seriously as to feel compelled to secure the amount of work for which his employees very naturally look to him. Some day we shall produce a class of employer which will rid the rest of the community of the menace of uncertainty now supposed to be inseparably associated with what is known as good trade and bad trade.

The employer, who is an employer, will see in time that his function is not only to make furniture but to make trade—a no less possible process.

However that may be, there is no secret which should be more earnestly regarded by every employer than the proper exercise of this right of discharging the employed. It will enable him to develop in the minds of the employed just that sense of security, the absence of which is the gravamen of the charge against the present system.

Controlling, as I do, a fairly large staff, it is impossible for me to have a personal knowledge of the qualities and capabilities of each member of it. But I reserve, and hope always to reserve, to myself alone the right of appointment and the right of discharge to and from the service of my business.

It frequently happens that the manager of a department will report that some subordinate is unsuited to his position and that he should be discharged. I never act upon such a report. I am thankful to know that each human being is a blend of peculiarities, and that we are not constituted in such a way that any two of us in all circumstances can always live happily together. The characteristic which may jar upon the susceptibilities of one manager may turn out to be a valuable asset in the eyes of another. Hence it is my invariable practice, upon receiving an unfavourable report upon an employee, to seek a second and a third report. A typist or a clerk or a traveller will be moved from the first department to a second and then to a third, and not until three departments have reported unfavourably do I exercise the right, which I possess as employer, of discharging a subordinate and creating unemployment.

In pursuance of the vague idea that I mention above, I have it to my credit that I have never discharged any employee of mine solely on account of bad trade. If things are slow in one department, they are probably active in another, and, in any case, my duty as a business man is to prevent business from being slack. I am not prepared to admit failure or shirk my responsibilities at the expense of others. There are, of course, some who must be sacked. There is the man whose ideas are bigger than his capabilities. He can learn his limitations only by moving from one job to another. In the course of time he will collect from various employers a sufficient number of opinions as to what are his real qualifications and will be a better judge of his own value. I have discharged people, and I hope I shall continue to do so, for bad time-keeping. One thing of which I am rather proud is my endeavour to establish a record in the matter of short office hours. My business constitutes a practical illustration of the folly of restriction and ca' canny. We work, omitting meal times (and I am referring now of course only to the clerical or manual class of labour), a week of $37\frac{1}{2}$ hours, and we try to cram into those hours every possible ounce of effort. We do not work on Saturdays and we are thus able to get into our lives a balance which is a very happy one. It is therefore my painful duty to exercise my prerogative of discharging those who fail to appreciate the advantages of this arrangement.

In my business, however, as I think in most businesses, there is to be found that security from unemployment which is so much talked about and so much sought after. It is, as it must always be, the result or reward of serious service. Equally, therefore, in theory, there can never be any unemployment for those who are willing to render such service. The great trouble, which we are not as a people really willing to recognise, is the insecurity of inefficiency. It is that trouble which drives so many workers to think well of schemes like nationalisation, which appear on the face of them to provide security without any apparent regard for efficiency.

This particular secret, the right understanding of one's obligations as an employer, leads me to look with grave doubt upon the modern fashion of organising industry into big units. The very large concern, controlling the output of some standard article and employing many thousands of workpeople, must, from its very nature, be liable to fluctuations from which the smaller organisation is immune. The huge combine, with a weekly wages bill as big as the whole of its annual profit, may be forced by adverse conditions to indulge in wholesale sacking to maintain its existence, and the menace of insecurity—always a feature of the industrial problem—is proportionately intensified. Of course there are great advantages in arranging matters upon such a scale as to secure the maximum output and the greatest economy, but it is possible that we may sometimes forget these, the only possible excuses for size, and carry the craze for bigness beyond the safety-point.

PARETO'S LAW: THE INEVITABILITY OF INEQUALITY

THE benefits of popular education, which, though we are apt to forget this, is an institution of quite recent times, are only now being felt. We are admittedly still experimenting with education, and it is as well to remember that the presence of thousands of millions of people on the earth who can read and write and think is an experience denied to previous generations, including even the Victorians.

This may be one of the reasons why we are all so actively and vigorously engaged in seeking new ways of living and exploring various forms of revolution, all of them quite untried and most of them necessarily unworkable.

A new world that can read and write looks back upon the old and sees in it much cause for complaint; impatient of waiting for that degree of knowledge and analysis by which alone it can understand the origin and nature of present evil, it sets to work in all its ignorance, with a fund of youthful enthusiasm, to put things right.

It would be amusing, were it not in some ways so serious, that a whole generation of people should flatter themselves that to them at last has come the revelation; that the world and the people in it from the beginning of time have been all wrong; that there was no wisdom in the past and that it has been reserved for us, the twentieth-century Olympians, to receive the gift of wisdom with an abundance denied to the long procession of our forefathers.

The next generation of economists will, in all probability, realise that the past is worthy of far more attention than it has hitherto received. Present-day writers on political economy may be divided into four classes. There are, first and most numerous, those who frankly set out to create some new social system; secondly, and less numerous, those whose researches and writings are designed to find fresh ways of raising the means, through taxation, to develop and extend the service of that modern fetish called the State. The third class is smaller still, and consists of those very rare creatures, the pure economists, concerned solely with the dry-as-dust science of analysing and defining the economic structure of society. Lastly, and this is the smallest class of all, comes the handful of writers on economic subjects whose object is the study and defence and extension of the existing order of things, who are impressed with the wonderful strides that have already been made in the difficult work of civilisation, and who believe that in the experience of the past are to be found the fact and the wisdom upon which the progress of the future may be assured. It is greatly to be hoped that this class will increase in numbers—a hope likely to be realised as the follies of the larger class of experimentalists become more obvious.

If the effort which is put into the study of new ideas could for a time be diverted to the study of the basis of the present order, so that we might be as thoroughly acquainted with the workings of what is called Capitalism as we are with the theoretical workings of some of the new systems, so eloquently recommended, we should acquire a practical proficiency in economic matters which is at present sadly lacking.

The eternal problem, the great single question, which is facing us and has always faced the human race, is the problem of the poor man. Our method of approaching that problem to-day does little credit to our intelligence. We see on the one hand a man who is poor, and on the other one who is rich, and we jump at once to the conclusion that the two phenomena are related, and that the solution of the difficulties of the poor man is to be found in the spoliation of the rich. We are helped towards that simple solution by a combination of the natural human instincts of pity on the one hand and envy on the other. A little more thought, deeper study, and a more genuine desire to get down to the real truth of the matter might bring us to the view that the salvation of the poor man is to be found in some scheme which would enable him to follow in the steps of the rich, and which would thus offer, or so it would seem, a prospect of riches for all, instead of what appears to be the only prospect held out by the other alternative—poverty for all.

The Italian economist and mathematician, Vilfredo Pareto, stands out among the more distinguished of those who have attempted serious work along these lines. Pareto's Law lays it down that:

(1) In all countries and at all times the distribution of income is such that the upper ranges of the income-frequency-distribution curve may be described as follows :—If the logarithms of income sizes be charted on a horizontal scale and the logarithms of the numbers of persons having an income of a particular size or over be charted on a vertical scale, then the resulting observational points will lie approximately along a straight line.

(2) In all countries and at all recent times the slope of this straight line fitted to the cumulative distribution (that is the constant m in the equation $y = bx^m$) will be approximately 1.5.

Pareto was an Italian economist who wrote much during the latter part of the last century and left behind him the law as to the distribution of wealth briefly stated above. I venture with great trepidation to suggest that, perhaps unconsciously, there has been something in the nature of a conspiracy to suppress Pareto. If he has come anywhere near the truth he disposes once and for all of any economic system based on Socialism. As we are all of us, from Diehard Tories leftwards, afflicted with a tenderness towards Socialism, which in some ways does us credit, no one seems to have thought it worth while to say much about Pareto. I cannot find (and I have made a serious search) a sympathetic explanation of Pareto's Law in the whole of the national economic literature. I discovered Pareto, almost by accident, through a very casual mention by Marshall in one of his heaviest volumes and an even more casual reference by Sir Josiah Stamp in his valuable work, *British Incomes and Property*. But no English writer that I have yet discovered has been at any pains to translate Pareto, or to give us an English version of Pareto's Law. The above summarised translation of the Law appears in a volume entitled *Incomes in the United States*, published by the National Bureau of Economic Research, New York—another illustration of American superiority in economic research and thought.

It must be said in extenuation of English economists that Pareto's Law is admittedly imperfect. It is based upon mathematics, an exact science, and Pareto has been found, indeed he found himself to be, unable to stand the searching cross-examination of the higher mathematicians.

Put into the simplest terms, Pareto's Law, if true, would prove that there must be degrees of wealth; that we must go up in stages, and that we all go up and down together; that economic equality is a scientific impossibility and that to raise the lower grades we must also raise the higher, or, vice versa, that in damaging the higher grades we cannot avoid corresponding damage to the lower.

It would appear to be universally admitted that Pareto's Law is true in so far as it brings within the terms of a definition the accumulated experience of the past. Those who hope for some new economic order are not prepared to admit that what has always been is necessarily a guide to what will be in the future. There is, of course, plenty of room for differences of opinion, but the point I desire to make is that the future would be easier, if not safer, if we had the advantage of a closer, more scientific and more thorough knowledge of the economics of the past.

All I can hope to do, for I am no mathematician, or indeed economist, is to tempt better qualified students to apply their minds to the doctrines expounded by Pareto. Would it not be possible, for instance, to begin a discussion as to the scientific possibility or impossibility of equality?

Forgetting economics, let us take some simple example that everyone can understand. Take, for instance, a heap of sand. Imagine the sand in an hour-glass, the small, smooth particles of which fall into their natural and ordinary position as more and more run through and are added to the pile. Such a heap will assume a conical formation; being widest at the base and having at its apex a single grain of sand. Its height will roughly be equal to the diameter of its base, and the largest number of grains will be at the base. For the sake of simplicity let us say that the heap has reached 100 grains of sand high and that there arrives another grain which desires to place itself on the very top of the heap. The heap will thus become 101 grains high, but, in order that the ambitious grain may remain at the top, it will be found necessary to add to the heap as a whole no less than 5,250 grains. 102 of these find themselves on the bottom layer and 101 will be deposited on the second layer from the bottom; 100 on the third layer; 52 on the 51st layer; 27 on the 76th; 4 on the 99th, and finally our ambitious grain will take its place at the top of the heap. In this simple exercise it will be demonstrated beyond possibility of doubt or misunderstanding that a single grain of sand, desiring to be at the top, has to arrange for 5,250 grains to be settled in appropriate positions below, and that the absence of a single grain at any stage lower down the heap will bring the topmost grain out of position. A similar little experiment could be undertaken with a few tennis balls. The conclusions to which it would lead would be the same.

If four tennis balls are arranged in the form of a miniature pile, three will be necessary on the bottom layer and one at the top. In order to make the pile higher, it will be found necessary to add three more to the bottom layer, two to the next and one at the top, and, further to increase the pile, we must add four to the bottom, three to the next row, two to the next, and one at the top. As the heap increases in height, balls must be added to each row in numbers varying in definite proportions to the height of the pile. Thus a single tennis ball, desiring to raise itself a grade higher, must arrange for the maintenance of a number of others in appropriate positions, and this would seem to suggest that one way at least of providing for the prosperity of the many lies in the encouragement of the enterprising and the ambitious. If it may be assumed by way of argument that there is some scientific similarity between the construction of society and the heap of sand or the pile of tennis balls, it would appear to be advisable to inquire a little more fully into Pareto and his law.

That the heap of sand is a good analogy seems to be demonstrated by the test of my own business. Many a small newspaper is produced by a proprietor-editor-manager with the assistance of an office boy and a clerk. The heap in that case takes the form:

Proprietor-editor-manager.

Office Boy.	Clerk.

As the enterprise develops and prospers, the heap grows; the number of grains in it increases, and it forms up somewhat as follows:

Proprietor.

Editor.		Manager.	
Reporter.	Typist.	Secretary.	Canvasser.
Sub-Editors.	Clerks.	Office boys.	Messengers.

When, in the course of time, the little paper becomes a big one, an enormous heap emerges, with the proprietor presiding over a board of directors, who in turn require the assistance of a news editor, a night editor, a foreign editor, a city editor, with corresponding grades of managers and publishers and, further down the scale, large armies of subordinates, all arranged in order of importance. The proprietor perched at the head of such an organisation will have much more to do than the little proprietor-editor-manager who produced his paper with the assistance of an office boy and clerk, and ought therefore to be blessed with a good deal more of this world's goods; but it appears that he can only attain such a position on condition that he makes and maintains numbers of other positions grading naturally down the scale, and that the solidity of the whole structure will depend upon the largest proportion of the benefits or proceeds reaching down to and remaining at the base of the undertaking.

It is, of course, admitted even by the Communists that there must be something in the nature of social status or grading. Thus an army is unthinkable without its due proportions of varying ranks from Field-Marshal to Private. If the heap of sand or tennis ball test is applied to the army it will be seen that a Field-Marshal cannot exist without a number of Generals, a larger number of Lieut.-Generals, a still stronger body of Major-Generals, who in turn require Colonels commanding battalions with appropriate Lieut.-Colonels, and so downwards through the company officers to the lowest ranks. The same kind of structure is to be found in a Church or in a Government department.

Thus it would seem to be the natural formation for society equally as for sand: all of which seems, to some extent, to justify Pareto.

It will be noticed that Pareto is very sweeping and very definite. He pronounces judgment upon all countries and all times, and he commits himself to a formula and a fraction which, although guarded with the word " approximate," are both very exact. Such discussion as has been concerned with Pareto's Law, and there is all too little of it, has centred round the slope of the straight line and the 1.5, and has succeeded in showing that 1.5 should sometimes be 1.3 or even 1.6. That is to say, that while Pareto gave us the line AB it has turned out that CD or EF may in some circumstances be the correct delineation.[1] But the difference in the angle of all these lines is immaterial to his general contention as to the distribution of wealth.

A still more complicated and technical discussion has ranged round the ends of the line, and nobody seems to be able to tell us with any degree of authority what really happens to the very very big and the very very

---

[1] See diagram 1, page 162.

L

small incomes. For these technical reasons, Pareto is at a discount among the higher mathematicians. That, however, does not seem to prevent them from making use of him for the practical everyday work of life, and, although we have apparently still to find an exact formula to cover the economic distribution of all

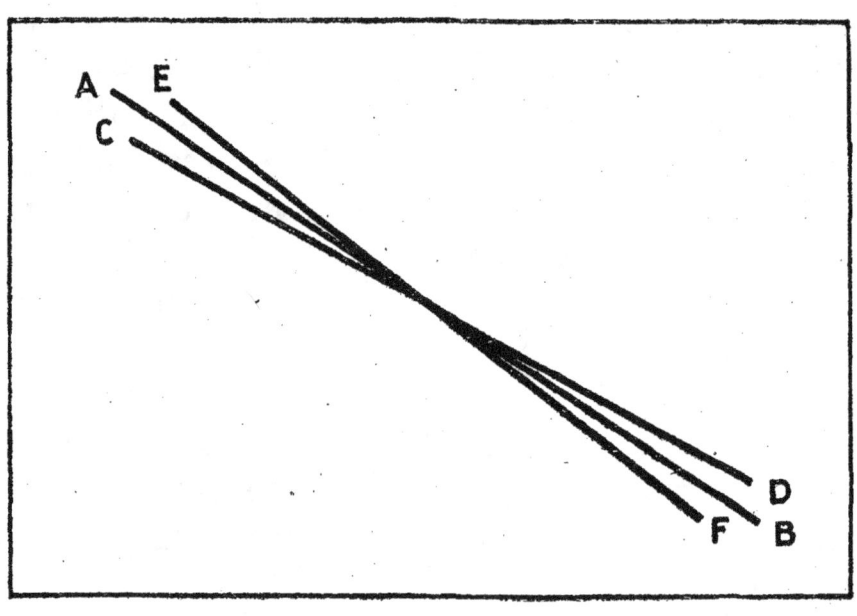

Diagram 1.

incomes, Pareto comes in handy in such a matter as the collection of taxes.

I understand that Pareto's formula is used by the Inland Revenue authorities, who graph their returns as directed by his law, and in that way profess to be able to detect any serious tendencies towards evasion and any serious flaws in their system of assessment.

Pareto therefore has his uses.

That being so, it would appear to be a profitable undertaking for others besides mathematicians and tax-collectors to look more carefully into the Pareto theory. If it is a fact that " in all countries and at all times " the income line runs as shown on Diagram 2, then whether the angle is 1.5 or 1.3 would appear to be a matter of detail which for the purpose of more general discussion can be safely ignored.

A hundred years ago we had a population of 8,000,000 and probably not more than a score of them with incomes approaching £10,000 a year. To-day we sup-

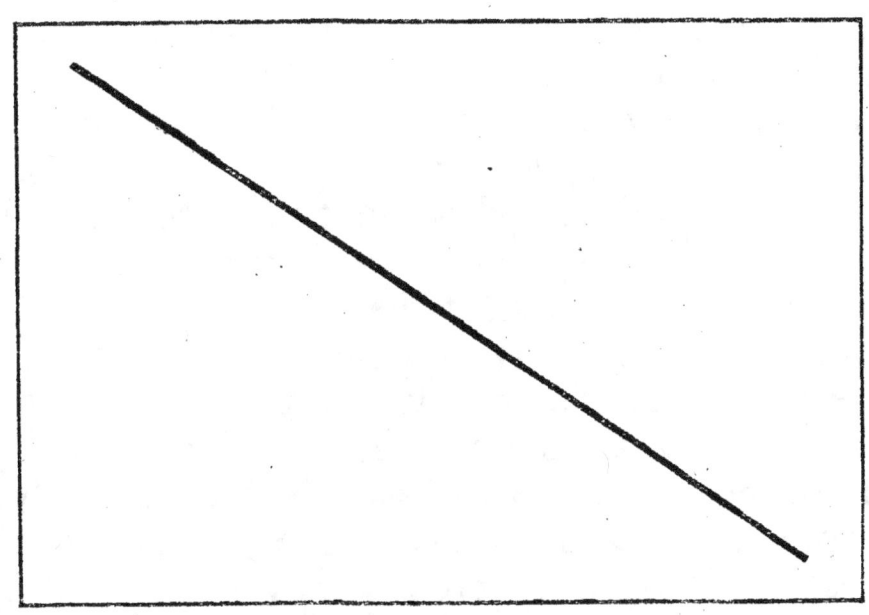

Diagram 2.

port no less than 47,000,000 souls, and Pareto would seem to say that it is therefore necessary for us to have at least some of our fellow-citizens in enjoyment of incomes of millions.

Applying the same theory at the other end, we get some economic light upon recent happenings in Russia. The wiping out of the wealthy would seem, according to Pareto, to require the physical disappearance of a much larger number of persons lower down the scale. And whether Pareto is right or not, that is undoubtedly what has happened.

Large numbers of our people believe that by taxation and legislation it is possible to approach equality of wealth; still larger numbers hold that by these means inequalities can be graded less steeply, while all hold that the burden should be regulated according to ability to bear.

Pareto would seem to say that these ideas are more attractive than workable, and to lead one to doubt whether the following of them is not in itself responsible for the slow progress of that general well-being which they are intended to promote.

If the increase of the wealth of the millionaires by 10 per cent. would mean a corresponding increase in the wealth of all of us, and is indeed a necessary scientific condition of our securing that improvement, then the sooner we know about it the better.

To advocate the encouragement of millionaires as a cure for social ills sounds a little out of tune with modern political thought, but, having regard to the failures of the immediate past, the idea is surely worth investigating. I am not concerned about the millionaires, but I do want more of this world's goods for the rank and file. If Pareto is right, we must have both or neither.

There is an opportunity here for a student of economics who will take up this question of millionaires and give us new light upon it. Everyone is interested in the millionaire, but interested only in his millions and what he does with them. Nobody seems to bother about the other millions which must necessarily have accrued to the rest of us before the millionaire could attain to his high position. If there is anything at all in my sand-heap theory it would seem that a good many thousands of millions must be distributed among us by anyone who succeeds in himself becoming a millionaire.

Guy Morrison Walker, in an interesting (if rather American) book called *The Things that are Cæsar's*, has a good deal to say on this subject:

Take the record of the life of James J. Hill, who constructed thousands of miles of railroad and opened up millions of acres of land that were formerly wild and inaccessible ; who bettered the conditions and raised the wages of hundreds of thousands of men and women by the opportunities for work that he created. Look at the cities, whose creation and growth he inspired, and the wealth and prosperity of a half-dozen states which his vision conceived and which his work made possible.

Which was the greater worker, a Roosevelt, who railed at swollen fortunes, malefactors of great wealth, and who sowed discontent and envy among the masses of the people, or a Harriman, who took the bankrupt Pacific railroads off the hands of the Government and by his genius for management and development not only recreated them and made them efficient servitors of the States through which they ran, but, by improving their service and reducing their transportation costs, brought prosperity to a score of States and increased the wealth of the people of those States which were dependent upon them, by a sum not less than twenty-five billion dollars ?

The fortune that Mr. Harriman left is a mere pittance compared to the wealth which he created for others. A commission so small when expressed in percentage of the money that he made for others, that if the ordinary man were offered business on the same percentage he would spurn it with contempt.

The foresight and courage of Commodore Vanderbilt in the organisation and consolidation of the original scraps of road and in the construction of the missing links that created the New York Central and Hudson River system, was what determined the leadership and pre-eminence of the State of New York in population and wealth in our country. Every man who is proud of the fact that the Empire State is the first State of our Union in population and wealth owes a debt of gratitude to old Commodore Vanderbilt. The paltry millions that fell to him were an infinitesimal part of the total wealth that his work gave to this State and its people.

. . . Our people have so long been relieved from the primitive methods of harvesting and are so ignorant of the use of the hand-sickle, or of the flail, or of the threshing floor, that they do not realise how much of labour has been saved and how much of wealth has been created for the farmers by the invention of harvesting machinery.

The money made by the harvesting companies is a small percentage of what their devices and machinery have saved not only the farmer but all the people who consume farm products; yet our people have been taught that the International Harvester Company is the last word in plundering practice, thievery, and unfair tactics.

. . . can anyone estimate the value of the services rendered to society to the world and the billion and a half of people in it, by Mr. Rockefeller, who, by making safe and cheap the use of petroleum and by building up an economical system of distribution, has spread the use of illuminants throughout the world, turned the night into day, banished ignorance and superstition, and done more to make possible reading and study, and the spread of education and culture, than all the men who lived in the world before his time ? Who can measure the value of the services to mankind of Thomas Edison, with his many inventions ? Or a Philip D. Armour, who, by the development of refrigeration and cold storage, has brought within the reach of the poorest in the land a quality of meat that was not only out of reach of the richest, but was absolutely unknown until he introduced his methods into the packing-house business ? Or who shall say what it was worth to the world to discover the method of refining sugar, that reduced it from its original cost of 25 cents, or a shilling, a pound, when that represented a day's work, to its recent price of 5 cents a pound, which, in our country at least, is not over one-hundredth of the wages for a day ?

If we could agree that we must all go up or down together; if it could be shown that it is impossible for anyone of us to go up or down without bringing the rest up or down with us, economic discussion would be very much simplified. Pareto shows us that this has always been the experience of the past, and, if it is to be the experience of the future, what a deal of trouble we could save ourselves by that knowledge.

The figures on page 167, giving the numbers of incomes of six different sizes which were listed by the Inland Revenue authorities in 1895 and in 1920, seem to support my contention.

It will be noticed that judged by money figures we have all of us been going steadily up. The number of persons with £3 a week has multiplied by 14, and the number of persons with over £50,000 a year has increased in proportion. The various classes have been multiplied by the figure shown in the last line of the table, and it will be seen that this varies from 14 to 12.

Increase in Numbers at certain Incomes

£160 to £300	£600 to £700	£800 to £1,000	£1,000 to £2,000	£10,000	Over £50,000
		No. in 1895.			
222,693	5,591	6,672	11,069	1,314	56
		No. in 1920.			
3,194,100	74,850	86,560	142,870	16,720	660
		No. of times increased.			
14	13.5	13	13	13.5	12

If Pareto's law is absolutely true, the multiplier should be 14 or 12 all the way through, and the slight discrepancy which my figures show points either to a weakness in Pareto or, as is much more likely, to a very natural inaccuracy in the Inland Revenue figures.

These figures do, however, demonstrate beyond question that twenty-five years of legislation which have included death duties and super-tax, which have seen the full development of the modern theory of placing the burden on the shoulders best able to bear it, which have reduced the public finances to the position in which two million persons are nominally paying the whole of the taxes, and which have led the wage-earning classes as a whole to believe that salvation is to be found through the spoliation of the rich, have, in fact, done nothing whatever to alter the slope of the line to which, so Pareto argues, we must all conform.

What has been happening is that while the poor have been getting less poor, the rich have been getting more rich, notwithstanding a political effort, unequalled in its force in the whole of history, to arrive at something pleasingly called equality.

If it should be a fact that inequality is inevitable; if

it may be admitted that society cannot exist except it be graded; if it is necessary that some of us must be on top and some below—and surely even the Communists admit all this—then the discussion reduces itself to the question: How best is this grading process to be performed; how best can the lower grades be arranged, so that each of us may fall naturally into the position in which we can function to the greatest advantage of ourselves and the rest?

Hitherto we have relied upon the process which may be described as the money test, the competitive system or Capitalism. That is only another way of saying that each of us has been subjected to the test of the opinion of our fellows. Under Capitalism every act performed by anyone of us is tested and found good or bad by the judgment of those whom it affects. Capitalism might be defined as the economic interpretation of the ideal democratic theory.

Discarding theory for the moment, we can, in the light of the experience of the last few years, look at the matter in a wholly practical way. We know, of course, that it is possible to select the higher grades of society as they have been chosen under the present régime in Russia. We know that there are serious students of Communism who believe that, by some system of training, super-men can be evolved who will naturally occupy the first positions in society. It is even suggested that we might resort to scientific breeding for the purpose of recruiting the necessary upper classes. But we of this generation have had the good fortune to enjoy practical experience of the workings of some of these principles, which should surely help us to form a sound judgment upon them.

I suspect that Fascism and Mussolini are not altogether unconnected with the writings of Pareto; a suspicion which does not strengthen the appeal of

Pareto to my democratic soul. It strengthens, however, my impression that there may be wisdom and experience to be found in Italy, of which we ought to avail ourselves if we are serious in our search for the best in economics.

I hope to see some such enthusiasm as that which brought Karl Marx out of Germany and built upon his writings a whole new literature of political economy, applied to the even more useful and promising task of unearthing Pareto from Italy and, on his foundation, building up a literature and a method of thought which will lead us to a constructive policy making for the general well-being of the whole community.

WHOM DO I ROB . . . ?

BACON, who must have been a poor judge of economic matters, said: " Property is like muck; it is good only if it be spread."

A consensus of opinion would, no doubt, declare that it would be better if an income such as mine were more widely dispersed. Most people would, for instance, argue that ten separate incomes of £1,000 a year would be better for the community than one income of £10,000 a year. Even those who are free from the folly of thinking that wealth is the cause of poverty, are many of them inclined to believe that a more level distribution of it would be for the advantage of all. Although the Communist agitator does not generally inform his audience of the fact, it is not unusual for men of my class and position to think seriously and deeply on these questions and inquire amongst ourselves how far, if at all, it would be possible to effect a more equal distribution of income. What good would arise if that could be done and what damage or loss would be incurred to balance the good?

" Whom do I rob?" is a question that I often ask myself. Could my income be better employed? Could it be more evenly distributed as between me and others? Could the people who work for me have it? Could it be spread over the customers, or consumers whom I serve? And, lastly, could my contribution, whatever it may be, to the general well-being be made without making my income?

The simplest illustration of the right distribution of income that I remember is to be found in the accounts of the North-Eastern Railway Co. before the War. The Company had an almost equal number of railway workers and of shareholders. Each shareholder had contributed on the average £1,500 of capital. Each worker received in wages an average of £75, and each shareholder received an average of £75 in dividends. It took, therefore, £1,500 of capital to find employment for one worker. The capital received the 5 per cent. which we have noticed in a previous chapter as the minimum inducement which will bring it into being, and the worker received the whole of the rest of the money which was paid by the users of the North-Eastern Railway. The most superficial examination of this position will show it to be completely sound and will indicate the only ways in which it could be altered. Any diminution in the £75 paid to the shareholders would discourage or stop the provision of any further capital for the North-Eastern Railway, whereas any increase in the money paid by the users of the railway could have been applied to the increase of the wages of the workers, and was, in fact, the only source from which any such increase could come. Had the workers, for instance, been willing to apply themselves to the use of labour-saving devices and to give twice the service with the same number of workers, or the same service with half the number, each man could have had double wages and with them acquired the spending power to employ the other half of the railwaymen in the provision of all the other things that the double wages would call on to the market. But I am not discussing railway wages. I merely give the above illustration as an introduction to the more detailed discussion of my position, and because it happens to state the problem with which I am concerned in the simplest possible way.

The most careful analysis of my own position drives me to the conclusion, to which I shall endeavour to lead the reader, that only one of two things can happen in regard to my own case. I can, through political action, be destroyed, wiped out, and shut up. My business and all the odd things that I can do can be dispensed with, and I freely admit that there is a great deal to be said in favour of this course. But it is equally certain that I cannot be replaced, that no agency other than the individual can ever do my work and that all the activities for which I am responsible must cease if I and my class are to be abolished, and incomes such as mine are not to be allowed.

The alternative, therefore, is to leave me with a freer hand to provide more wages and employment than I now do. Keeping my illustration of the North-Eastern Railway in mind, my position may be stated in similarly simple terms. Income, £10,000, derived from a turnover of £400,000. Every year a large number of persons who think they like such matter as I publish pay to me of their own free-will the sum of £400,000. Of this money I pay away to workers and to others £390,000, and retain for my trouble the £10,000 which is the cause of all this discussion. I take 2½ per cent., or 6d. in the £. To be fair and exact, it should be pointed out that I really take 1¼ per cent., or 3d. in the £, for my personal use, and another 1¼ per cent., or 3d. in the £, for the benefit of the Chancellor of the Exchequer. But without going into that, because, of course, I should be the first to vote for the abolition of the Chancellor and all his extortion, it may be said that I charge 6d. for handling a sovereign. My 6d. can be divided in another way, and I may claim that I charge 3*d*. for providing £1 in wages to those who work for me and another 3*d*. for the delivery of £1's worth of books and papers to those for whom I work. It would be very easy to develop the argument that my remuneration is far too small to be really good for the general community. I ought, so some people think, to make a very much higher percentage on my turnover, so that I might induce competition, offer a more brilliant example and more serious temptation to others to come along and provide work and goods as I have done, a temptation which is not offered by a paltry 6*d*. in the sovereign.

In these days, when the whole of the machinery of politics is concerned with the provision of the thing called " work," I am providing work at a cost to the wage-earner of 3*d*. in the sovereign. I distribute wages on a far lower expense ratio than Old Age Pensions are distributed. Unemployment pay costs much more to hand out over the counter of the Labour Exchange than I charge for handing out wages to the large number of persons who have become involved in the enterprise which I have built up. The best-managed insurance office costs 10 or 11 per cent. in the simple business of paying out death benefits, and I pay wages in life, a much more difficult operation, for $1\frac{1}{4}$ per cent. I should plead guilty were I charged with damaging the community by earning far too little money and being in fact, in a dangerous form, a price-cutter.

My second inquiry was whether my income could be more evenly divided. It seems, on the surface, obvious that this could be done, and that it would be good if it should be done. To take an extreme case. I receive £200 a week, and one of my office boys gets 25*s*. a week, out of which he has to help a widowed mother. The widowed mother is, in these modern days, as useful in argument to the Socialist as she was in my younger days, when in political discussion she always appeared as a brewery shareholder. Surely no damage could be done to anyone if I, being a well-disposed person, conscience-smitten with the disparity between my position and that of my office boy, decided that he should have £10 a week and that I should manage to struggle along with the £190 left to me? But such a superficial proposition needs to be examined rather more carefully. It will be noticed that in taking 3d. in the £ from my wage-earners as I do, I am taking 3¾d. a week from this particular office boy in respect of such service as I render to him by providing, or arranging, or being the instrument through which his 25s. a week is secured. Put the other way round, if the office boy is really pulling his weight, doing his share of the total of the work of my organisation, he is providing me with 3¾d. per week, and the other £199 19s. 8¼d. which goes to make up my income belongs, if it does not belong to me, to all the colleagues of the office boy in proportions calculated at the rate of 3d. in the £ on their individual wages.

It is, of course, a duty and a pleasure now and again to help some boy who, for reasons with which every one is familiar, has fallen a victim to one or other of the many troubles that beset the human being. Notwithstanding the fact that the Chancellor of the Exchequer takes exactly half my income and professes to deal with these same troubles, I find from experience that he does not do so, and that I am constantly called upon to give a helping hand in one direction and another. The trouble here is that such help as one is able to give, notwithstanding a big income, is not more than enough to assist a fraction of the cases of distress which come under one's notice. I do, however, get a small degree of satisfaction from the thought that the few hundreds

a year which I am able to give away does a great deal
more real good than the £5,000 a year which the State
takes from me in the name of distress, which it generally fails to alleviate. It will be noticed, therefore, that
if I only give my office boy, with his 25s. a week,
another 3¾d., I hand over to him my share of the
business in which he and I are jointly engaged. If
I give him 7½d., I hand over to him the share of some
other office boy as well as his own.

My third inquiry, as to whether the worker could have
my income, would thus seem to be disposed of. It is
suggested that, in the ideal state, the workers will employ the capitalist instead of the capitalist employing
the workers. Mr. Sidney Webb has taken great pains
to elaborate this idea. By ignoring losses and concentrating on a few outstanding cases of excessive profits,
he does not find it difficult to show how he thinks the
workers could employ capital at a lower rate of remuneration than it occasionally secures. I venture the
assertion, however, that if my 3d. in the £ were the
rule, as it undoubtedly is the average, it is totally and
utterly unthinkable and impossible that wages could
be secured in any state of society, or under any system,
at a lower cost than this which I charge. Many of the
wage-earners who work for me could, however, secure
a very great deal more than they now have if they
would direct their attention not to my income but to
my £400,000 turnover. In the larger sum there is
ample room for rearrangement and reorganisation,
forty times as much room, in fact, as in my paltry
£10,000. It is beyond dispute that in taking the
whole of the latter, my workers could only add 3d.
to every £ they now receive, whereas many of them
could without trouble take twice as much as they now
take out of the £400,000 which comes through my
bank account in the course of the year. The most

obvious way in which this can be done is by realising the effects of trade union practices and restrictive regulations.

There is a sum which cannot be stated with any exactitude, which I put at a minimum of £50,000 a year, that is absolutely wasted, poured down the gutter or thrown into the air, by all those multifarious arrangements with which I am surrounded, and which either forbid men to work or, which is far worse, stop machinery from working. The extent to which this wholly foolish idea has been developed in these days is a chief cause of any lack of wealth from which any of us are suffering.

Most printing works have to carry on their business at the dictation of at least fifteen trade unions, each union having its own rules and regulations, and each concerned with its own rights and privileges.

Idleness by rule, enforced with all the powers of the union, may appear to produce wages, but it cannot produce any wealth. It does not even distribute wealth. It merely keeps back the progress of the race.

The destruction of wealth, brought about by arrangements of this kind, is not confined to the many absurd objections to machinery and speed. A circular was recently issued to a number of my employees by a printing trade union in the following terms:

"DEAR COMRADE,—I am writing to let you know that we are in dispute with Messrs. X, and you are to use every effort to see that supplies are not handled for this firm.—Yours fraternally, ——, General Secretary."

I do no business with Messrs. X so far as I know, but the circular in question, sent to every member of the trade union concerned, will undoubtedly have reached many houses which are in business connection with Messrs. X. The members of the union are not informed what is the nature of the dispute. They are not invited to exercise any discretion in the matter. They are given no opportunity of expressing a view with regard to it. They are not allowed to discuss the matter with other employees; but an arbitrary power, working in the background, more far-reaching and destructive in its operations than any power which was ever known in the days of slavery or feudalism, is able not only to punish Messrs. X, but cause thousands of workers in hundreds of other firms to delay and destroy wealth-production at the expense of the whole community.

In case it should be thought that I am guilty of some exaggeration, it may be well to mention some of the most obvious effects of this kind of thing upon my business. I have handled in my time some scores of publications, mostly weekly trade papers. The following is a list of papers which I have discontinued, enterprises which have been killed, and several of which would have been running to-day if printing prices had remained at the 1914 figure. That figure is, of course, an impossibility, and the real economic price of printing should probably be somewhere between the present extortionate figure and its 1914 equivalent. Among the many papers which I have been obliged to stop are :

The Goldsmiths' Review.
Farm and Home.
The Argentine Trader.
The China Clay Trade Review.
Kelly's Monthly Trade Review.
Tools.
The Retail Trader.
The Order Book.
The Japan Trade Review.
The Leather Goods Review.
Commercial Intelligence.
Ways and Means.
The Egyptian Trade Journal.
Australian Markets.
Indian Markets.
South American Markets.
The Transport World.

This little list could be enlarged indefinitely, if an examination were to be made into the position of the trade paper business before the War and to-day. My

M

turnover might be double what it is, my income might be double, and there might be another £400,000 available in wages, if only the printing trade would allow the machinery which is at its disposal to work. To a large extent these people still look upon the machine as did the Luddites. There is many a small trade paper and many more small papers, concerned with small subjects and small causes, which could be rendering useful service to their own particular little circles, if they could be produced for a matter of £50 or £100 a week.

The printers to-day have only left room for the big things, and the big things are not always the best things. While therefore there is, I claim, nothing to be got for the workers out of my £10,000 a year, there is a great deal they might have, if they would direct their attention to the £400,000 a year which I handle. The abolition of my £10,000 would necessitate the discovery of some agency to take my place, an agency sufficiently solid and reliable to be able to provide regular wages and the security which I cannot offer for less than the 3d. in the £ which I take.

This brings us to the next of the questions which I set myself to answer. Could my income be given to my customers? Could it be applied to the reduction of the price of the commodity which I sell? If the whole of it were so given there would, of course, be nothing for the workers to argue about, and there would be no revenue for the Chancellor of the Exchequer. On this question I need not go into the detail that I have devoted to the subject of the workers. Much as I love my customers, and much as I desire to serve them, I may be permitted to remark that I am not prepared to hand on to them a sovereign's worth of material which I produce for their benefit at a lower commission than the 3d. which I charge them for so doing. As a matter of fact, I am working for my customers on a dangerously low scale of remuneration. When my father, Sir John Benn, reached the most profitable stage in the career of *The Cabinet Maker* as a monthly publication, he was working on a very small turnover and a profit of 25 per cent. *The Cabinet Maker*, monthly, with a revenue from subscriptions and advertisements of slightly over £5,000 a year, enabled him to enjoy an income of £1,200 or £1,300. By publishing weekly and by publishing ten journals instead of one, by further sifting out ten strong journals from a long list of weak ones, I have built up a business of much larger dimensions and have reduced the rate of profit to one-tenth of his figure, a fact which, as I have suggested, might constitute a much more serious charge against me than any which can be fabricated out of my supposed exorbitant income. This again illustrates what Socialism has done for the printing and publishing businesses. It has wiped out the chances of the small enterprise and reduced the public to reading the big things. *John Bulls*, *Daily Mails*, and *Hardware Trade Journals* are all very well in their way, but they deny to numbers of serious thinkers and writers the opportunity of communicating their thoughts to their fellows, opportunity which rests with the printing trade to give.

There is another way of looking at all this. Leaving out figures of turnover or of income, leaving out the stereotyped discussion of production and ca' canny, is it for the good of the human race as a whole that I should be allowed to carry on at all my particular kind of business? Does the human being become a better human being because of the existence of *The Gas World* or *The Hardware Trade Journal*, or the volume which I publish entitled *The Synthesis of Nitrogen Ring Compounds*?

Of course the world could get along without these things. Similarly the world could exist without tobacco; it would probably be better if there were no such thing as a hat; it is conceivable that human life might be tolerable without wireless—some people are firmly of that opinion. This is a line of argument which leads us to the still more reasonable conclusion that the world could do very well without me and without nine-tenths of its population—an ideal which, when reduced to its simplest terms, is the real aim of the Socialist. We could run this earth on one-tenth of our numbers, with the simplest forms of food and shelter ; and we are doing our very best, by the stopping of machinery, by rules against work, by waste and destruction, and the prohibition of human effort at every turn to achieve that end.

If, on the other hand, it is desirable that we should multiply, that we should keep ourselves occupied, that we should develop our minds in such ways as are rendered possible by discussion of nitrogen ring compounds, the peculiarities of tobacco, and by experiment with wireless, then we must recognise that such enterprise as that for which I am responsible and such activities as those which I control, are the only ways of achieving those ends; that we can develop indefinitely in these ways and can secure much more wealth than we have ever yet dreamed of; that we can multiply wages and go on for ever adding to human enjoyment, if this is human enjoyment, only on such lines as those which I have described.

The industrial ideal which embodies prosperity of this kind is composed of four elements; four elements which are always found in combination, which must all be recognised, and which cannot for long exist one without the other. They are:

1. High Production.
2. High Wages.
3. High Profits.
4. Low Prices.

There is no case of real industrial success in which any one of these four elements has been absent, and the attempt on the part of any party or any theory to deny the utility of any one of them, or to secure any one of them without reference to the other three, has never yet failed to lead to disaster.

TAXATION AND PUBLIC EXPENDITURE

In speaking of an income of £10,000 a year, I feel guilty of practising something in the nature of a deception upon the reader. Except to the 10,270 persons who, to use the official phrase, are " in the enjoyment of " an income of £10,000 or more, the discussion of my financial position so far must almost of necessity have led to a great deal of misunderstanding. The reader with £500 a year very naturally imagines me to have twenty times his income, £20 for every one which he possesses, and carries that simple proportion through all his ideas as to what I can afford in comparison with himself. To those with smaller incomes still the disparity is even greater. It is a natural and a pardonable fact that most people are quite unable to conceive of any limitations to the enjoyment or power or freedom associated with an income stated to be £10,000 a year.

Human experience is to a large extent disillusionment, and in this matter of income we discover at the end of a successful endeavour to secure a coveted position or prize that our ideas as to its quality or value have to be much modified. £10,000 or rather more is what I call my " taxit." It is the amount figuring against my name in the national accounts. It is added up by the statisticians and economists and duly recorded as part of the nation's income. It goes to form part of the glorious picture so skilfully painted by those whose self-imposed mission it is to educate the poor with regard to the wealth from which they have been disinherited; but it is in no real sense an income. I believe my real income, my actual profit, to be, in 1914 figures, something less than £3,000. As nearly as I can calculate, I am now in the position, so far as purchasing power is concerned, that I should have been in in 1914 with an income of £3,000 per annum.

The injustice of stigmatising me with a £10,000 income is the more cruel having regard to the fact that a very large proportion of this money never comes into my hands at all. I am not even permitted the luxury of receiving it and handing it over to the Chancellor of the Exchequer. By the process of taxation at the source, the person in my position receives 15s. and is required by Act of Parliament to call it £1. He is also required to pay further taxation upon this fictitious pound. Almost half my income goes in direct taxation. The official rates—income tax, 4s. 6d.; super-tax, graduated up to 5s.—I do not reach the 6s. mark—do not quite amount to 50 per cent. of one's income. As most taxpayers will appreciate, actual income and taxable income have a way of varying, and the variation does not operate in favour of the taxpayer, so that of my £10,000 my bankers are only troubled with the handling of £5,000. Another big slice is taken from me through local imposts and indirect taxation.

I have, as we all have, to suffer the effect on prices traceable to taxation. Although I admit there is room here for complicated and difficult argument, I put the cost to me of local and indirect taxation at another £2,000, thus bringing my real position down to the more modest qualification of a £3,000 man. For present purposes it is sufficient for me to state—a statement which no one will attempt to controvert—

that I bring home and myself spend far less than I actually pay to the Chancellor of the Exchequer and his satellites.

Taxation has been defined as " the art of so plucking the goose as to secure the largest amount of feathers with the least amount of squealing." That definition is as true to-day as it was when Colbert used it in the seventeenth century. He knew nothing of income tax and super-tax. The methods of his time for securing the feathers without the squealing were confined to the imposition of indirect taxes placed upon such commodities as appeared to render them least obvious. The modern method for reducing the squealing is altogether different. It is not so to spread the taxes over the largest numbers that they are not readily recognised, but to reduce the taxpayers, or the nominal taxpayers, to the smallest possible numbers, well knowing that the louder they squeal the less will be the attention paid to them. I recognise that it is no use squealing, and, in any case, I have no particular admiration for the squealer. This problem of taxation is a question of the public good and nothing else. I flatter myself that I possess enough of the qualities of the good citizen to believe that, if it is in the public interest that we should spend large sums upon labour exchanges and a base at Singapore, it may well be in the public interest also that half my income should be taken for those purposes. But it is permissible to point out that there may be a danger of obscuring what is really and truly in the public interest, if the public is befooled into thinking that its interests can be secured, not at its own expense, but at the expense of a small body of insignificant persons like myself. Twenty-two million electors express by a majority their opinion that a Singapore base is desirable. That opinion would be a more serious one if each of these twenty-two million

electors, when giving it, were fully conscious of the
fact that each of them would have to bear his or her
proportion of the expense of the enterprise. The value
of the opinion may be, and is in fact, vitiated by the
common and altogether fallacious theory that the expense is met by taxation imposed upon me and the
small number of persons in the country in my position.

Out of the whole population there are rather less than
two and a half millions who pay any income tax at all.
Assuming that every income taxpayer has a vote, it
follows that barely one voter in ten has any sense of
direct financial responsibility attaching to the exercise
of his franchise rights. The heavy taxpayers, the
people who have considerable sums to pay, are less
than 90,000, this being the number liable to super-
tax. Those who pay on the scale which applies to me
number only a paltry 10,270 persons. So that the
futility of anything in the nature of squealing becomes
obvious. Super-taxpayers are just about as numerous
as the inhabitants of the Isle of Wight, or Wigan, or
Rochdale, from which it may be deduced that any
agitation on their part, or any squealing by them,
would carry just about as much weight with the nation
or with Parliament as some grievance, however keenly
felt, of the estimable persons who happen to have their
homes in one of these delightful places. As to my
own class, the unfortunate ten-thousand-pounders,
they would, as persons, be rightly regarded by the
nation and the Empire as of equal importance with
the inhabitants of the Laccadive Islands, their numbers almost exactly corresponding to the population
of these important territories. To wipe out my class
completely, to remove from the stage (as has been
done in Russia) persons like me would, from a personal, a liberty, or an individual point of view, be
exactly as important as the wiping out of the white

population of Bocksburg, and I confess that, one Britisher being as good as another, I should have no more reason to squeal at being wiped out than would the least important of my Bocksburg fellow-citizens.

Squealing will not help my argument. The nation must have the maximum of feathers and there must, no doubt, be a certain amount of squealing however they are plucked. That brings the argument on to much firmer ground—that of the public good. We are led to inquire whether the public good is really being secured by the present rates of taxation and public expenditure. National expenditure during my business life has, of course, grown enormously, as will be seen by the following table, which, even after making allowance for differences in money-values, still shows an enormous increase for which it is difficult to find justification.

Growth of National Expenditure

					£
1890	...	...	...	...	...	86,000,000
1899	...	...	...	...	...	127,000,000
1906	...	...	...	...	...	160,000,000
1914	...	...	...	...	...	207,000,000
1923	...	...	...	...	...	969,000,000

These figures do not tell the whole story, because between 1890 and 1923, local expenditure, which at the earlier date was almost negligible, has grown to a proportion which makes it to-day a heavier burden than was the whole of the national expenditure thirty years ago. In considering the enormous figures which are now believed to be necessary, we have to remember that at least £300,000,000 a year must be collected and distributed as War Debt service, the price which we have to pay for the calamity of 1914-1918. So far as the rest of our public expenditure is concerned I take the view that the great bulk of it is largely wasted. It is spent, I know, in pursuit of objects which are mostly good, but objects which we shall learn only by experience are not to be achieved this way. Whether, however, we achieve the objects by public action in greater or lesser degree, it will be generally admitted that such action is expensive and wasteful. In 1914 the expense to the Exchequer on account of education was £19,169,647. In 1922 the Exchequer paid out under this heading no less than £65,909,000. These figures represent only a portion of the cost, that portion which falls upon the national Exchequer. It cannot be pretended, indeed I have never heard it argued, that we were enjoying $3\frac{1}{2}$ times as much education in 1922 as in 1914; nor is it suggested that education was $3\frac{1}{2}$ times as good in 1922 as it was in 1914. It must, I fear, be admitted that the addition of nearly a million a week to the national school bill which has taken place in a short period of eight years is in large part due to the elaboration of machinery created and maintained in deference to the modern faith in system and organisation.

The national accounts in the last few years have swollen, and will continue to swell, not on account of the extra work which is done for the nation's benefit, but on account of the introduction of the military mind into the arrangement and direction of national affairs, aided and abetted by the Socialist idea that there is some virtue in creating a job, quite apart from the product that comes out of that job. I remember a distinguished Colonel in command of a training camp on the South Coast who turned down a proposal for a telephone from one part of his command to another on the ground that the orderlies would then have nothing to do, an excellent example of the principles upon which we conduct our public business.

A further instance is provided by the Board of Trade:
" We have given some consideration," says the second
Geddes Report, " to the organisation of the Board of
Trade, and are particularly struck by the fact that
although some of the operations of the old Commercial Department of the Board now form part of the
functions of the separate Department of Overseas
Trade, the part of the Commercial Department re-
tained has been expanded into three costly specialised
departments, namely, the Industries and Manufac-
tures Department, the Power, Transport, and Economic Department, and the Commercial Relations and
Treaties Department."

Wherever one looks in the national accounts the same
tendencies are evident. The Board of Works spent
£3,621,378 in 1914. In 1921 the figure was
£12,607,000. In 1922, in spite of the Geddes Report,
and notwithstanding falling prices, the figure was
£14,702,655.

This is not some bureaucratic conspiracy, although
were I to attempt to deal with it on the lines of the
critics of Capitalism it would not be difficult to build
up a theory of the greedy, bloated bureaucrat fattening
in idleness on the work of the people. I know too
much of the Civil Servant, and have too high a regard
for his qualities and his energies, to indulge in this
kind of abuse. The Civil Servant is a victim of his
circumstances. He is struggling with a system which
never has, which never will, and never can, work.
Red tape is not the invention of an idiot. It is an
absolute necessity in the performance of public work.
The remedy is the reduction of public work to the
barest minimum. Public work cannot have the advantage of individual responsibility behind it, and thus
must be performed with the handicap of rule, regulation, and red tape, which must always render it both

inefficient and expensive. It is, for instance, stated that the windows of Buckingham Palace are cleaned on the inside by the Office of Works, and on the outside by the Department of Woods and Forests. Whether that be so or not, it is obviously right and proper that it should be so. The taxpayer could have no confidence in the correctness of public accounts which allowed one department, in the exercise of its own discretion, which might be wrong, to trespass upon the preserves of another.

Since the Ministry of Munitions led us all astray, even private business has suffered terrific harm from the " system " mania. The City, as well as Whitehall, is still full of flappers filing futile forms. Though the City is beginning to recover from the illness, Whitehall can never recover from it. The remedy is not to allow the latter to dispense with necessary system, but to recognise that Whitehall is an unwieldy, clumsy, and expensive instrument, and to reduce its functions to the essential minimum. The disease of public expenditure and activity springs, however, from other causes.

Herbert Spencer, with a prophetic knowledge, the quality of which was little appreciated at the time, told us all about it in *The Coming Slavery*. He wrote:

" A comparatively small body of officials, coherent, having common interests, and acting under central authority, has an immense advantage over an incoherent public which has no settled policy, and can be brought to act unitedly only under strong provocation.

" Hence an organisation of officials, once passing a certain stage of growth, becomes less and less resistible; as we see in the bureaucracies of the Continent.

" Not only does the power of resistance of the regulated part decrease in a geometrical ratio as the regulating part increases, but the private interests of many in the regulated part itself make the change of ratio still more rapid. In every circle conversations show that now, when the passing of competitive examinations renders them eligible for the public service, youths are being educated in such ways that they may pass them and get employment under Government. One consequence is that men, who might otherwise reprobate some further growth of officialism, are led to look on it with tolerance, if not favourably, as offering possible careers for those dependent on them and those related to them. Anyone who remembers the numbers of upper-class and middle-class families anxious to place their children, will see that no small encouragement to the spread of legislative control is now coming from those who, but for the personal interests thus arising, would be hostile to it.

" These various influences working from above downwards meet with an increasing response of expectations and solicitations proceeding from below upwards. The hard-worked and over-burdened who form the great majority, and still more the incapables perpetually helped who are ever led to look for more help, are ready supporters of schemes which promise them this or the other benefit by State agency, and ready believers of those who tell them that such benefits can be given, and ought to be given. They listen with eager faith to builders of political air-castles, from Oxford graduates down to Irish irreconcilables; and every additional tax-supported appliance for their welfare raises hopes of further ones. Indeed the more numerous public instrumentalities become, the more is there generated in citizens the notion that everything is to be done for them, and nothing by them. Each generation is made less familiar with the attainment of desired ends by individual actions or private combinations, and more familiar with the attainment of them by governmental agencies; until, eventually, governmental agencies come to be thought of as the only available agencies." (" The Man *versus* The State ": The Coming Slavery.)

It is to the causes so accurately diagnosed by Herbert Spencer that we must attribute the existence to-day of such useless institutions as the Ministry of Labour, the Ministry of Transport, the Department of Overseas Trade, the Mines Department, the Petroleum Department, to mention only those the abolition of which was definitely recommended by the Geddes Report less than three years ago.

We badly need another such report to save us from the error of accepting these abuses from habit, for they are fast becoming very bad and deep-rooted habits. That Mr. Winston Churchill, with the backing of a Conservative Government, should standardise national expenditure at eight hundred millions emphasises the seriousness of the present position. I am conscious that it may appear that I am squealing because my money is being spent in these ways, but, as I shall presently show, I am not at all sure that it is my money which is being so spent. For, notwithstanding all the intolerable taxation, I have more money than ever. I am much more concerned with the harm that these absurd departments do, quite apart from the money that they cost. Every one of them stands in the way of individual action and personal initiative, and every one of them constitutes at innumerable points a discouragement to those who would be glad to get along with the work of reconstructing the world and supplying the needs of mankind.

Public expenditure must, from its nature, be wasteful. It is as well that we should recognise that inherent weakness in it. State work tends to be done at an uneconomic price, a well-known fact which is widely recognised but little understood. This difficulty does not arise from greed or avarice or chicanery on the part of public servants. The trouble is deeper seated. It arises from the fact that in public work, as distinguished from private work, there is no real test of service. If private work is bad, private persons decline to have it. The test of competition, the freedom of choice, the checks on extravagance, and the incentives to betterment, which are essential elments of private business, are absent in dealings with a public body. A bad piece of work sold to a private person brings discredit on a private trader and robs him of future business. A bad, useless, or extravagant piece of work sold to the public is invariably blamed upon the politicians.

A great deal might be written about the injustice of taxation; the unevenness of the burden; the way in which it presses more hardly in some quarters and more lightly in others. But there is really very little in this kind of squealing. Taxation, like any other public action, must be inefficient, unjust, and uneven. There is no more injustice about taxation than about any other big public scheme, which can never, from its nature, fit itself to all the many variations of individual circumstances. As will be noticed by reference to the figures I have given of the early profits of *The Hardware Trade Journal*, I was paying income tax long before I ever had a profit. The following simple illustration shows what happened to me and what happens to every man who starts in business:

Taxation upon a New Business subject to the Three Years' Average

1st Year ... Loss,	£2,000	... Assessment,	Nil.
2nd Year ... Loss,	£500	... Assessment,	Nil.
3rd Year ... Profit,	£500	... Assessment,	Nil.
4th Year ... Profit,	£1,000	... Assessment,	£333
5th Year ... Profit,	£1,000	... Assessment,	£833

Total Profit, Nil; Total Assessment, £1,166

It is argued that this injustice is balanced by the operation of the average later on in the account, when profits are rising more rapidly than the assessment for taxation. Those who press this point overlook the fact that any advantage secured in this way is often more than balanced by the taxing regulations which forbid the calculation of many expenses in estimating profits. These are many and complicated. The cost of repairs in excess of some fictitious statutory average is not allowed. Large sums are collected from traders on the strength of the regulation which says that " losses not connected with, or arising out of, the trade in which they are engaged may not be set against profits." The list of liabilities which the trader has to bear and which are not allowed as trading expenses has been growing for years, and continues to grow, a fact which, together with the steadily increasing powers of the taxing authorities, tends to make taxation ever more oppressive and unjust.

" Some writers on economics," says Ireson, " evidently with no practical knowledge of accountancy, have assumed as a matter of course that the official statistics form a true record, in no way exaggerated, of the income actually received by payers of income tax. This assumption has been shown to be incorrect. It will be understood, of course, that what is challenged is not the textual accuracy of these statistics, but the popular use of them for a purpose for which they were never intended. They do not agree, and were never meant to agree, with ordinary accountancy results, and in certain respects it is quite proper that they should not so agree." (*The People's Progress.*)

" . . . Official statistics are . . . misleading, *i.e.* they do not recognise any loss of capital which has been suffered by the tax-payer. . . . Losses from bad investments, or from unsuccessful trading, in so far as they result in the exhaustion of capital, are also ignored. Assume, for example, that I invest the sum of £1,000 equally in ten different companies. In the first year nine of these pay me dividends at the rate of 5 per cent., while the tenth company goes so hopelessly wrong that my investment in it must be treated as totally lost. Thus for the year I receive £45 in dividends, and lose £100 of capital, the actual result to me being a *loss* of £55. Nevertheless, income tax on £45 has to be paid, and in the official figures I appear as having made in that year an income, *i.e. a profit*, of £45. It is no exaggeration to say that the example just given is representative of thousands of others occurring every year. All around us, in every trade, capital is being destroyed in various unsuccessful ventures, yet no notice whatever of such destruction is taken by the Revenue authorities, and there is absolutely no record of it kept by them. When there is a profit, it is sought out, assessed, and taxed, but when there is a loss of capital the income tax officials pass it by as if it had never occurred. No one would accept as reliable the statistics of a general who published the achievements of those of his soldiers who survived, but suppressed all mention of those who were killed. Everyone would agree that such a record was misleading. For a precisely similar reason the income tax returns are misleading, for they include only the profit of successful ventures, and suppress all mention of those which destroy capital when they fail and die." (*The People's Progress.*)

N

The sense of injustice in connection with taxation is created and fostered in another way. The taxpayer is perhaps beginning to understand that he must pay upon losses as well as upon profits, but there is a new and a deeper resentment against taxation which arises from complications that are beyond the power of almost any taxpayer to understand. This is in some measure due to the several new forms of tax invented as a result of the bigger demands of the War. It always seems to me that it should not be beyond the power of the taxing authorities to make their calculations and their demands a little more intelligible to the victims. I profess to know something about figures; I am supposed to be a fairly good judge of accounts; but I admit myself totally unable to understand some of the calculations upon which my taxes are computed.

A recent experience which befell me is worth quoting as some excuse for my confessed ignorance. My business became liable to excess profits duty. I shall go to my grave with the feeling that I never made any excess profits, within the meaning of that term as discussed in Parliament and by the public, but I have long ago learnt to ignore Parliamentary discussion upon details of taxation. My accountants and the authorities agreed together that I was liable for some years for fairly heavy payments of excess profits duty. I paid. But when the duty was abolished and the last accounting period was reached, my patience was exhausted and I kicked at a final demand for the last year, amounting to £6,500. The demand was doubly offensive to me, partly because I had no £6,500 readily available, but also, and more definitely, because I objected to the stigma attaching, and rightly attaching, to a man found liable for £6,500 on account of excess profits made by reason of the nation's difficulties arising out of the War. My accountants went into the matter with Somerset House. A stack of papers, which could not be read in a month, was accumulated. Calculations were made, and arguments adduced which would have conveyed just as much to my intelligence had they been written in Greek. It was agreed that I must pay this £6,500. I was not satisfied and took the exceptional course of consulting a second firm of chartered accountants, who had the reputation of being experts in their knowledge of the workings of the excess profits duty. A further stack of papers was slowly accumulated; further arguments were brought forward on either side, and I received an assurance from these experts that the demand was proper and correct, and that I had no alternative but to pay up. I was still unsatisfied, still unhappy (as indeed might be expected) about the whole business and decided to consult yet further experts. I employed, therefore, another well-known City firm of chartered accountants. All this professional assistance cost money, but this time I was rewarded. After going through the usual process, and using another hundredweight of ruled foolscap, another decision was reached. I do not profess to understand anything about it ; I only know that in so far as the Chancellor of the Exchequer made the purpose of the excess profits duty clear to Parliament and to me, I was never intended to pay any such duty, but I did have the satisfaction of receiving, not a demand for the payment of £6,500, but a Treasury Warrant for £500, repayment of duty now admitted to have been collected in error in respect of previous years. I tell this little story not because of any interest in the details of it. It is a story which could be capped by many thousands of traders up and down the country, but I press it because of its bearings on the question of taxation and justice. I suggest that it is not just, not

O*

expedient, and not good for the State or the body politic that taxing technicalities should be developed to a point where the taxpayer is reduced to a helpless cypher in the hands of experts, and where he finds himself at one moment asked for £6,500 and a few months later receiving £500 on the same figures and the same facts and the same position, being all the time totally and absolutely ignorant of the ways in which, the principles upon which, or the figures by means of which these results are secured. The loss of confidence in the Treasury and the State engendered in the minds of commercial men by these methods is not only detrimental to business, but harmful in the highest degree to the State itself.

I once paid 26s. in the £ on a part of my income; a thoroughly unjust imposition which I do understand and which, because I understand it, I do not resent to anything like the same extent. A large slice of my income is derived from a commission on the profits of the company over which I preside. The reader will remember the arrangement made in 1901, when I cancelled my original shares in the Hardware Trade Journal, Ltd. In some of the small type of the many taxing Acts of Parliament passed during the War it was provided that a director's commission should not be allowed as an expense in calculating profits for the purpose of taxation. Out of consideration for the peculiar views of the Socialist Party, directors, presumed to be the agents of Capitalism, were singled out for a special form of treatment in this way. My commission did not amount to as much as the commission paid to some of my managers, but your Socialist will admit that a manager may earn his commission, while no director can, of course, earn anything. So that, at the height of War taxation, a portion of my income was added back to the profits of my company and was

assessed to excess profits duty at 80 per cent. My
company, therefore, paid £1 of commission to me and
16s. of E.P.D. to the Exchequer. The £1 which I
received was liable to income tax at 6s. and super-tax
at 4s., and I, in my personal capacity paid these sums.
There was only one sovereign; that was admitted. It
formed part of the profits of my company which were,
under my contract, payable to me by way of commission. In respect of that sovereign, the Chancellor of
the Exchequer collected 16s. from my company and
10s. from me. The remedy for this injustice was, so
I was informed, in my own hands or in the hands of
my company. The Act provided that, although the
company was liable for the 16s., it was empowered to
recover that sum from me, and had I been willing to
repay that amount to the company and be content with
4s. income instead of £1, I should then only have been
charged with 2s. income tax and super-tax instead of
10s., on a gross income of 4s. instead of £1. Seeing
that my contract with the company was of very long
standing, and seeing, moreover, that my family depended upon the commission which was properly mine,
I did not see my way to renounce my contract or my
commission, and, as I have said, the result was that
for a period of a year or two a part of my income,
some £2,000 or £3,000, actually produced to the
national Exchequer rather more than 20s. in the £,
the loss falling upon the shareholders in my company.

These little things are unimportant in individual
cases, but, multiplied as they are into thousands of
others, they give rise to an attitude of mind towards
this question of taxation which is in every way to be
deplored. Instances of this kind could be multiplied
indefinitely, but there is one other point that may be
mentioned even at the risk of appearing to squeal. It
is quite impossible to earn or win anything in the

nature of a character with the taxing authorities. The
business man who behaves himself moderately well
can build up a character in the course of time. He
may reach the position where a bank will grant him
accommodation merely upon his name. He will certainly reach a position where his colleagues in business,
other firms the world over, will take his statement as
conclusive evidence of the correctness of figures, however much they represent. No such reputation is ever
obtainable with the taxing authorities. I have for over
thirty years been in close communication with those
who are responsible for collecting my income tax. In
the whole course of all those negotiations and all that
period no question has ever arisen as to my integrity,
as to the correctness of my figures, as to the fullness
of my return, and no suspicion, so far as I am aware,
has ever attached to me of an attempt at evasion or of
an unwillingness to discharge obligations properly laid
upon me. Even so, after thirty years, no simple, unsup-
ported statement of mine is admissible in connection
with matters of taxation. I must fill up every form;
I must give every detail; I must recapitulate every
item. No such thing as a character is known in public
affairs. I may be marked up in the highest grade in
every inquiry office in the world; I may be classified
by the merchants as worthy of any credit; I may win
the highest position among my fellows; but I can
never get a good mark of any kind from this thing
called the State.

The tyranny of the taxing machine and the growing
lack of confidence in its workings are enhanced by the
feeling that Parliament has less and less to do with it,
and that it is becoming more and more a matter of
bureaucratic discretion. A couple of illustrations will
show what I mean. When Mr. Asquith, as Chancellor
of the Exchequer, first introduced a discrimination

between earned and unearned income he was asked in Parliament as to the position of the small family company. It will be remembered that income was divided into " earned " and " unearned," so that rather more taxation might be placed upon the shoulders of those whose incomes were derived from mere owner-ship. It was felt, and there is a good deal to be said for the feeling, that an income arising from a dividend on a share should be taxed at a higher rate than an income which was the result of personal work and effort. Parliament was anxious that this distinction should be a true and not a fictitious one, and debated the position of the small family limited company. There were and are many thousands of small traders who, for the convenience of accountancy and for simplicity in the settlement of family interests, run their businesses as limited companies, although the shares are entirely held by fathers and sons and brothers actually working in the businesses themselves. That was in fact the position of Benn Brothers, when Mr. Asquith went to some trouble to explain to Parliament that the heavier taxation on unearned income would not apply to dividends earned by such companies as these. He gave the most categorical assurance that the dividends of persons actually working in small limited companies would be regarded as earned income. So definite was this undertaking that the Chambers of Commerce went to the trouble of issuing a circular to explain to small tradesmen that such dividends would be taxed at the 9d. as distinguished from the 1s. rate. When, however, the Finance Act for the year came to be finally passed and printed, no reference was made to this under-taking, and from the first introduction of the distinc-tion all the profits made by little shopkeepers who happen to have taken advantage of the Joint Stock Companies Act have paid at the higher unearned rate.

Another illustration of this same trouble was afforded by the Budget and Finance Act of 1924, introduced by Mr. Philip Snowden. Reference to the Parliamentary debates will show that Mr. Austen Chamberlain brought forward an amendment providing that sums placed by limited companies to a development fund, and not distributed as dividends, should be taxed at half-rates, upon the understanding that if at any future time such sums were distributed by way of bonus shares or capitalised in any other way, they would then pay the full rate of the current income tax. The arrangement was a very proper and useful one. It removed an injustice widely felt and gave an incentive to trading concerns to build up reserves and thus ensure future development. The amendment was accepted by Mr. Snowden, and the House of Commons was left with the impression that the thing would be done. The Finance Act of 1924, however, contains no reference to the matter. Parliament has been overruled by some higher authority behind.

I am quite convinced that the taxing machine is the most efficient thing we possess. The troubles of which I complain are due to the difficult nature of the work that it has to do—extracting the national revenue, which reaches a figure in total and a figure per head of population neither of which has ever been approached in the history of mankind, and both of which are far in excess of anything it is possible to attempt in any other country.

It is not a convenient thing to be in correspondence with fifteen surveyors of taxes at one time, but that has been my experience. I admire the skill and pertinacity of each of the fifteen, although I confess that I have not always been able to maintain a perfect equanimity of temper with every one of them. If a man in my position happens to have the good fortune to earn a few sovereigns outside the district in which his income tax is usually collected, a new member of the Inland Revenue staff will pounce upon him and will require all sorts of declarations as to the total amount of his income set out on the numerous pages of the various big forms, in the detail with which most readers will be familiar. It is, as a rule, possible to satisfy these hard-working servants of the public with the name and address of the colleague who is looking after one's account, but that does not always settle the matter. Some years ago a friend of mine persuaded me to take a seat upon the board of directors of a small company which wanted my advice. Meetings of the board were held once a month, and the directors' fees were a guinea a meeting. The secretary of the company, in accordance with the requirements of income tax law, promptly sent my name to the surveyor of taxes with the information that I was entitled to £12 12s. a year in fees. Thereupon I was assessed at 5s. in the £ on £12 12s., and the appropriate officer in this case was not satisfied with my statement that the amount went into my general account, and that I could be relied upon to pay the tax as part of my general total. I referred him to my own local surveyor, but, from an examination of the papers, it did not appear that I had specified this particular company in the long schedule of my previous emoluments. That was perfectly true. I have so far succeeded in satisfying the assessors with detailed information on all items of £20 and upwards, and I finish my taxation account with a convenient entry which I call " sundries," which includes all oddments of this kind. Thus the surveyor was justified in claiming that these directors' fees were not duly scheduled in my income tax returns, and he, therefore, pressed a separate payment in his own district in respect of them. I sat upon that board for some eighteen months; I attended only five meetings and received in fees £5 5s., but the local tax-collector, good fellow that he was, with his intimate knowledge of averages and the year before and the year after, and statutory income, assessable income, taxable income, and actual income, adding these things together and dividing them into first instalments and second instalments, extracted from me in all over 2½ years £6 17s. 1d. income tax on my five guineas in fees. I am quite aware that I might have put the matter right had I been willing to spend a great deal of time explaining that, although I had been returned by the secretary of the company as entitled to twelve guineas per annum if I attended twelve meetings per annum, I had in fact only attended five meetings in eighteen months. Or I might have got out of the whole business by elaborating still further my complete return to my own surveyor in my own district. But there is a limit to the time a business man can give to these things. I estimate my time to be worth £5 an hour and it actually pays me better to submit to a demand for a few odd sovereigns than to give the time that would be required to argue the matter with my official superiors. Your income tax official, like every official, has no time sense. It does not matter to him how many weeks he spends in collecting a few shillings so long as the system and the principle are right.

We have in Great Britain attained a standard of honesty and proficiency in this matter of taxation which is unequalled in any other country of the world. I believe that to be a very precious asset which we should be at great pains to preserve. While there is, no doubt, a certain amount of tax evasion by a minority of persons, we English, in conformity with our commercial traditions, and assisted by our highly-developed sense of citizenship, do, in point of fact, pay our taxes with a correctitude which is absolutely unknown in any other part of the world. The Frenchman who evades taxation enhances his social position. The German and the American are not quite so bad, but no Englishman can gain any credit from his fellows by reason of defalcations in the payment of taxes.

But the high rates at present prevailing, and the oppressive methods which they render necessary, are developing a new mentality in the individual towards public obligations which is much to be deplored. We are busy encouraging the habit of legal tax evasion in a way that will cost us very dearly in the future. It is a regrettable thing from this point of view that the National Council of Social Service, a body with the highest motives, should be able to issue a circular (N.C.S.S. 29) containing elaborate instructions to taxpayers as to modes and methods whereby they can so arrange matters as to double their subscriptions to charities at the expense of the Exchequer. The super-taxpayer who is willing to give £50 a year to a charity can, it appears, through the agency of the National Council of Social Service, increase his subscription to £100 a year without adding to his expenses. This is a typical example of the evil that follows in the wake of high taxation. It is very natural, very understandable, and is bound to occur if we must have such high taxes as those which now oppress us. I do a little legal evasion, and I suppose everybody in my position is forced into the same sort of thing, in the effort to make my income perform a mere fraction of the things that are expected of it. I am bound to consider the effects of taxation upon each of my transactions.

Here is an illustration of the expedients to which one is driven. I own a house which, if let, would produce me an income that would be subject to income tax and super-tax. I am also blessed with an impecunious friend whom it is my duty to assist. I therefore put the friend into the house rent free. I make a contribution to his income, nearly half of which comes out of Treasury funds, and the house pays taxes through my poor friend on the lowest possible scale.

Or take a case that I believe will become historic when its details are known and its implications are thoroughly understood. Sir Alexander Grant handed over to Mr. J. Ramsay MacDonald, when Prime Minister, 30,000 preference shares which, it is stated, were to be held by Mr. MacDonald during his life, on condition that he willed them back to the Grant estate.[1] Sir Alexander Grant was very properly and generously desirous of easing the personal financial anxieties of a man of modest means who found himself in the onerous position of Prime Minister. But, when the transaction is examined from the taxation point of view, I conceive it to be possible that a large portion of the assistance given to Mr. MacDonald may in fact have come out of the coffers of the Treasury.

My only point, and it is a simple but important one, is that such things as these are sapping at the roots all our standards of taxation honour, and are developing a mentality towards public obligations which is highly undesirable.

Perhaps the gravest aspect of our present taxation position is to be found in the frightful discouragement which high rates and oppressive regulations offer to new enterprises. It is not too much to say that they must, from their nature, kill initiative and damp down at the source much new development which would be very helpful to us as a nation. The

[1] I understand that since the publication of my first edition, these shares have been handed back to Sir Alexander Grant.

case of the young man who would start in business is rendered ten times more difficult to-day than at any previous time, and in England more so than in any other country.

My purpose in stressing this question of taxation is to bring the public conscience back to a realisation of the depths of the plight into which war and war's aftermath have landed us. There is a very large section of the public which looks upon taxation as good in itself. Some people, and they are all too numerous, look upon the taxation of the rich as a proper punishment for being rich. If this view could be sustained and justified, there might be something in it. But so far from really acting as a punishment to the rich, taxation, as at present arranged, can, I think, be shown to be nothing more nor less than a fraud on the working man.

It is commonly argued that, while local rates enter into the cost of production of commodities, Imperial taxation does not. The old economists showed conclusively that when the income tax was varying from 8d. to 1s. in the £ it did not in fact exercise any influence on the cost of commodities. It may, however, be necessary to reverse that opinion in the light of recent experience. The old economist never considered the possibility of taxation running up to 10s. in the £. When income tax stood at 1s. I do not remember a single case where a manufacturer or merchant took taxation into account in considering costs and selling prices. To-day it is, I think, true to say that no business of any kind is undertaken until the bearing of taxation upon it has been fully investigated. The taxpayer himself is subject to the grave inconvenience of finding large sums for the Exchequer and does all the grumbling, and for the most part he is no more conscious of what I believe to be the truth than is the non-taxpaying public, that the bulk of high taxes is added to the cost of goods. We have reached a position where the taxpayer is really the tax-collector. I regard myself, not as a payer of taxes, but as the conduit pipe through which the State receives large sums that I collect from other people. Sir Jesse Boot showed beyond question that this was true of excess profits duty, and I am inclined to think that it may also be true to a large extent of income tax itself.

Whoever pays the taxes, however, there is another way of looking at the matter. The taxes are spent for the benefit of all. Even if it were possible to collect them at the expense of a minority, it is not possible to spend them for the benefit of a minority. Parliament has never sanctioned the expenditure of a single penny-piece except for the reason that such expenditure was in the national interest, and we are all concerned with that. Even such a costly blunder as war itself is never undertaken except upon the excuse that it is essential in the interests of the whole nation. From this it follows that it is right and proper to consider the income of the State as the income of its citizens, and to give credit to each citizen for an equal share of the State's expenditure.

Now the Treasury and the local authorities are between them responsible for the expenditure of £3 per week per family, taking the average family as a man and wife and three children. If this money is wisely spent; if it is really spent in the interests of the nation irrespective of class or party, every father of a family receives his due share of the benefits which come from this expenditure; so that it may be said that the Chancellor and his satellites do in fact expend on behalf of each family amongst us £3 each Saturday. It would be useful if we were, as a public, to concentrate our attention upon this expenditure per family and the benefits which we receive in respect of these disbursements, and ignore for the moment the more complicated argument as to who really pays. I would, if I had my way, take steps to bring home to every father of a family the real nature of the benefits which he receives from all this public money. It would, I think, do much to develop a real sense of citizenship and a degree of personal responsibility in these matters, which is woefully absent so long as we go on thinking of public expenditure as paid by the rich. When I receive a dividend, there is attached to it an explanatory note, which sets out the gross amount of the dividend, the appropriate amount of taxation, and calls my attention to the reason for my receiving a smaller sum than has actually been earned by my investment. I am thus constantly reminded of the " benefits " which I receive as a citizen through the activities and disbursements of the public authorities. I propose that a similar plan should be adopted in the payment of wages. I would print a pay envelope in something like the following way (I take the case of a labouring man receiving £2 10s. weekly):

					£	s.	d.
Wages	...	...	...	...	5	10	0
Stopped by the Exchequer			...	...	3	0	0
		Balance		...	£2	10	0

The labouring man Saturday by Saturday would thus have his attention called to the fact that in addition to the £2 10s. which he took home to his wife, he was also receiving at the hands of the numerous officials appointed to look after his needs and his comforts in many various ways, the equivalent of another £3, thus making his total income £5 10s. Such a plan could not fail to stir a public interest in this question rather more intelligent than it can at present claim to be.

Gilbert rendered immortal the man who might have been a Russian, a Turk, or yet a Prussian, but in spite of all temptations remained an Englishman. If Gilbert were alive and writing to-day he would, no doubt, elaborate this theme, and remind us, in a way we could all understand, not only of the advantages of our nationality, but of the price we pay for it. To be an Englishman is, of course, worth any sacrifice, but we are nearing the point when Englishmen themselves are entitled to inquire whether the charges associated with the privileges they enjoy are all of them necessary and reasonable.

The examination of the rates of taxation in different foreign countries and in our colonies discloses some very startling differences. Mr. McKenna, in a speech to the shareholders of the Midland Bank, stated that we were the most heavily taxed people in the world; a statement which, to the minds of his hearers, suggested a difference which might be measured in small percentages. As a matter of fact, the Englishman with an income of £5,000 a year pays more than double the income tax and super-tax which would be levied upon him in the next most expensive place on earth, France.

In presenting the following figures it is necessary to utter a word of caution. The comparison between the taxes of various countries can only be of a rough-and-ready kind. The circumstances in each country are different, the method of assessment is not the same in all respects in any two, and various complications make the following figures unreliable in detail. Nevertheless, the margins disclosed in the following table are so big as to leave no possibility of error in the general conclusions that can be drawn from them.

Table showing the Income Tax and Super-tax Payable on Incomes of £2,000 and £5,000 in the following Countries:

	Income, £2,000	Income, £5,000
	£	£
Great Britain	600	1,787
France	200	838
Norway	240	600
U.S.A.	146	526
Denmark	130	500
Sweden	160	400
Australia	142	736
South Africa	92	270
Holland	65	213

It will be seen from the above that a man with £2,000 a year can change his nationality and move to Amsterdam and add to the income, which he spends as he chooses, rather more than £10 a week; the man with £5,000 can improve his financial position by no less than £1,500. This piece of information is not likely to cause a run on the office which issues naturalisation certificates for Holland, because most Englishmen would agree that in spite of all temptations they will retain their nationality. The Dutchman, however, contemplating settling in this country, will find the difference in taxation a powerful deterrent.

The point was brought up to date by a statement issued from the Treasury dated February 28th, 1924, which set out the tax burden per head before the War and in 1923-24 in the leading foreign countries and in some of our dominions (see table, page 210).

That ever-growing section of society which is interested in the question of peace and entertains the hope of abolishing the habit of war might add some very

Treasury Statement issued by the Chancellor of the Exchequer, and dated February 28th, 1924. Tax Burden per Head:

—	1913 or 1913–14 (actual). In sterling at par			1923 or 1923–24 (estimated). In sterling at par		
	£	s.	d.	£	s.	d.
United Kingdom	3	11	0	15	18	0
France	3	7	0	6	18	2
United States (Federal) ...	1	7	11	6	14	10
Italy	2	2	8	3	6	11
Germany (Reich)	1	10	8	4	1	4
Canada (Dominion) ...	3	8	2	7	19	8
Australia:						
(Commonwealth) ...	3	8	1	8	1	9
(States)	1	5	11	3	4	2
South Africa:						
(Union)	1	9	0	3	9	11
(Provinces)	0	4	9	0	11	9
New Zealand	6	3	0	12	5	3

powerful arguments to those which it ordinarily uses, derived from an examination of the effects of war upon taxation. Nobody can now deny that in war the victor pays. It is clear to the whole world what has long been clear to the student of economy, that it costs more to win a war than to lose it. These simple truths are obvious to any who will look at the relative financial position of the victors and the vanquished in the 1914-18 War. What could be more illuminating than the spectacle of the nations of the world, acting through the League of Nations, imposing an obligation on the defeated Austria so to frame her normal budget that her maximum taxation shall not exceed a rate of £2 per head of population? Consider Great Britain, suffering from an actual tax burden of £22 per head and possessing all the advantages supposed to attach to victory, insisting, as one of the punishments which must be inflicted on the vanquished, that they shall be let off with a burden of one-eleventh per head of the taxation that the British citizen is carrying. We now know, which was not clear at the time, that the much-vaunted fruits of victory really consist in the privilege of taxing ourselves eleven times as heavily as those who are deprived of these fruits. Along these lines, the believers in the possibility of ending war might do much more to further their cause than can possibly be done by some of the arguments to which they give greater prominence.

In concluding this chapter, I desire to repudiate once again any intention on my part of attacking the officials whose duty it is to administer the financial affairs of the nation. I have had, perhaps, as much experience of, and personal contact with, surveyors of taxes and tax-collectors and clerks to special commissioners, and all the rest, as most living men, and I have never failed to find them, as persons, helpful and courteous and desirous of assisting. The trouble is not with the men who work the taxes; it is in the unworkable nature of the machine as a whole. Like all big things, it must be clumsy and cumbersome and, in detail, inefficient. If it could be seriously contended that all this taxation was for the good of the people as a whole, then no squealing by me or by anybody else would be entitled to a hearing; but since it can be stated that the maximum in taxation has in fact coincided with the minimum of national prosperity, squealing or no squealing, there is a *prima facie* case for further inquiry.

We have a bad way, we English, of attributing our troubles to causes beyond our control. We are invited to believe that our unemployment, our bad trade, our low standard of living, are the direct outcome of the state of affairs in Russia and in other remote parts of the world. My suggestion is that a further understanding of these matters may lead us to appreciate that the main cause of the majority of our troubles is the modern mania for invoking public action, for taking money which would be productive and useful if left in private hands, and rendering it sterile and useless in the dead hand of the State machine.

LargePrintLiberty.com

Dedicated to offering books on libertarian thought and economics in Large Print paperback.

Titles include:

For a New Liberty, by Murray N. Rothbard (Philosophy)
"A classic that for over two decades has been hailed as the best general work on libertarianism available. Rothbard begins with a quick overview of its historical roots, and then goes on to define libertarianism as resting 'upon one single axiom: that no man or group of men shall aggress upon the person or property of anyone else.' He writes a withering critique of the chief violator of liberty: the State. Rothbard then provides penetrating libertarian solutions for many of today's most pressing problems, including poverty, war, threats to civil liberties, the education crisis, and more."

Principles of Economics, by Carl Menger (Economics)
"In the beginning, there was Menger. It was this book that reformulated, and really rescued, economic science. It kicked off the Marginalist Revolution, which corrected theoretical errors of the old classical school. These errors concerned value theory, and they had sown enough confusion to make the dangerous ideology of Marxism seem more plausible than it really was. Menger set out to elucidate the precise nature of economic value, and root economics firmly in the real-world actions of individual human beings."

Great Wars and Great Leaders, by Ralph Raico (History)
"In the backdrop of this blistering and deeply insightful and scholarly history is the whitewashing of 'great leaders' like Woodrow Wilson, Winston Churchill, FDR, Truman, Stalin, Trotsky, and other collectivists. They are highly regarded because they were on the 'right side' of the rise of the state. But do they deserve adulation? Raico says no: these great leaders were main agents in the decline of civilization in the 20th century, all of them anti-liberals who used their power to celebrate and enhance state power."

www.ingramcontent.com/pod-product-compliance
Lightning Source LLC
Chambersburg PA
CBHW080410290526
45791CB00008BA/2214